my
Jo
Love Jo

ISBN0967365309

02000

9 780967 365305

Jo

I believe all wonderful stories should start with "Once upon a time." The following story isn't fantasy, even though some parts seem so miraculous that I could have made them up, but this was my real life with **Jo**. It was almost as if I asked God to let this magnificent girl fall in love with me; let her be gentle, understanding, and make me happy. I didn't ask, but I did receive. Songs influenced young people of my time and when I first saw **Jo**, my first thought was, "you must have been a beautiful baby cause, baby, look at you now." From that instant on my life revolved around **Jo**.

I was too young to know what I know now; it was too marvelous to be reality at the time. It seemed like a remarkable dream. It took the following stories and maturity for me to understand that love is a many splendored thing and true love grows year after year.

Jo's journey through life was enriched for everyone who knew her. She was a perfectionist in her heart and her soul. In my case she became the most important person on this Earth. She was the best wife I could have prayed for. In my Dad and Mother's life she was the most astounding daughter-in-law that they could have ever wanted; they both told me so over and over again. " Ken," they would say, "how did you find this marvelous girl? We love her so much."

Words can't say how much I loved **Jo**. She was joyous when you felt joy, she hurt when you hurt, but if she felt pain, you would seldom know it. She only wanted to shine if it wouldn't intrude on anyone else. With **Jo** as my partner, how could I not enjoy each second here on earth with her? I wanted to say the right words about how much I loved her, but couldn't, wanted to give it a number, but only God could know a number that large.

Jo

She wasn't an actress, she didn't play a part, and was herself at all times. **Jo** always looked and felt much younger than she was, because of the great care she took of herself. When she had to give her age to a nurse or doctor they would question her, thinking she was much younger.

No job was beneath her, no goal was ruled out. I ruled out some things and stopped her, because I feared she might get hurt. I felt that was my job as her husband. We would talk it over, add our love and move on. Life has its ups and downs, but love was our greatest common denominator; between us love was always involved.

I felt as **Jo's** husband that I had to protect her all her life. This world had a lot of pitfalls- a wrong turn, or heading down the path that leads into trouble might hurt the one you love. I couldn't take a path that might lead to trouble that would hurt my **Jo**, the girl I loved so much. The affection I had for **Jo** was always on my mind. I looked for the pleasure that she would give me when my love enveloped her. I couldn't say anything that might hurt her.

Jo made life so wonderful; she loved life so much and that is the honor she gave to everyone who knew her. She put something of herself in everything she did – her love. Her love expressed itself in how she wrapped gifts at Christmas time, how she picked cards, how she cooked, how she planned to help others. Touching everything so genteelly. Her devotion enveloped me and together we had the good times I write about. I want to relive the time I had with my **Jo**.

God is so proud of her he knows how good she was, a role model all her life. I feel sure that God would want you to know about my **Jo** and try to live your life as much like she did as you can.

I was like a child at play
waking up with Jo each day
She could spark me into action
I was sure of satisfaction
Just knowing Jo was around
was cause for my feet to leave the ground
Love, I was sure, was on it's way
it came in the words that Jo would say
Hearing her voice
was cause to rejoice
"Hi, Ken," she would say
and those two words made my day

When I First Met Jo

Even from a distance, **Jo** was attractive, slender, with beautiful, thick, wavy hair. As I approached her, I saw she had soft, blue eyes, beautifully arched brows, and a smile that you knew was sincere. She was 105 pounds of God's magnificent creation and I thank God every day for giving me my **Jo** for over 50 years.

Dating **Jo** a few times, I know now that I was obsessed with her from the start, justifiably so. I'm sure that I was jealous of **Jo**, but when I told her that, she would just say in that soft, sweet voice of hers, "Aw, Ken, don't worry about that. I'm yours and you're mine forever." My heart would just melt; **Jo** had that effect on me for the rest of my life.

Jo never told me anything that wasn't true. I always said, " I don't worry about you. It's the guys who see what a good thing I have with you that worries me." Again she reassured me that nothing and no one would come between us, and it was true for all the years of our married life. **Jo** knew how much I loved her, and being such a wonderful person, she overlooked some of my faults and returned some of my love for her back to me. She wrote in her diary that if anything happened to me she didn't want to live. In the depths of my heart, I feel the same way. **Jo** took great care of what God created, mentally and physically. She was against anything bad and for everything good. It takes a lifetime to understand. She saw the bad and walked away from it, saw the good and walked towards it – no smut, no drugs, and no violence; just friendship, honor, loyalty, and love.

When I first met Jo
I was drawn to Jo like a magnet
that pull I would never forget
We rejoiced in our attraction
two of us with a loving reaction
Each night when we departed
feeling almost broken – hearted
Looking forward to our next meeting
love improving with each new greeting
Talking to Jo, I had found true love
being blessed from the heavens above.

A Chance Meeting

It's a joyous time in my life. I have the best Mother and Dad on this earth. My health is good and I have no problems with school. I'm working for Dad, more coins in my pocket than I know what to do with. I'm popular at Church, have so many friends, my cup runneth over.

I was about 17 years old when I started fussing with my hair, running around so happy, not knowing what I was doing most of the time. My mother knew from the way I was acting that it had to be because of a girl. I told my mother I was spending a lot of time at the Conery, the place where **Jo**, who was about 16 years old, was working most of the time. I even pointed it out to her one day while we were out driving. I was so excited; I told her all about my wonderful, beautiful **Jo** and the Conery.

In our day, the meeting place for young people was an ice cream parlor or a confectionery in a drug store. You could order a coke or ice cream, buy candy or a sandwich, and set in a booth nursing your purchase until your friends showed up. That was the place you could wait in comfort, talk, and arrange what you would do in the next few hours, while greeting the boys and girls you palled around with.

The Conery was not near **Jo's** home; it wasn't on a route she would normally travel. My friend, George, had moved a block from the Conery, so we made one trip to get some ice cream. "Once upon a time," a glance at a beautiful girl and my life was changed forever, God knows for the better. **Jo** standing behind that counter was what I desired, above all. The most refined creature I'd ever seen. **Jo** was a lady in girl's clothing. I had seen thousands of girls and movie stars on the silver screen, but nothing like this, I was stunned. It took my mother to explain that this feeling was real love, the same she had felt for my dad. When I saw **Jo** I couldn't stay away. I can't remember how it happened, but we came together forever. I thought I wasn't good enough for her, but God blessed me, giving me **Jo** forever. I saw her for the rest of my life. Everything I did was for this, attractive, amazing, young girl. I took her home from this part – time job and we became full – time partners forever. Thank God for little girls.

Entered an ice-cream parlor by chance
not knowing my life would be enhanced
Seeing **Jo** stirred my emotions
finding everlasting devotion
You can't imagine how I felt
Jo caused my heart to almost melt
That continued for over 50 years
so much love and so few tears
Jo was perfection
in every direction
Left and right
into the night
I was never without **Jo** until now
I can't change the past only God knows how
To make it right for ever and ever
I'm sure God's plans will bring us together

One evening as I was sipping a Coke in the back booth of the Conery, I looked up to see my mother standing there before me. She was

Leta

dressed up for a party that she and my dad would be attending; he was in the car outside waiting for her. She looked magnificent as she handed me a note and told me, "Have a nice night. See you later." I stood up to watch her leave and only then did I realize that the whole place was bustling. Everyone was looking at and speaking about my mother.

What's wrong with these guys? That's my mother! I knew she was pretty, but I felt only my dad and I were allowed to acknowledge that. **Jo** rushed over to me, all excited, and said, "What a gorgeous mother you have." She continued to say how the silk dress, pearls, high heel shoes, and hat were so attractive on my mother, and that her hair had been done so beautifully. Mother must have been about 32 then, and dad was 36.

When I drove **Jo** home from the Conery that night, she was still talking about how my mother made such a big impression in such a short time. She said all the girls who were in the Conery couldn't stop talking about how exquisite she looked.

Soon after that, I took **Jo** home to meet my mother and dad. When I went into the service after graduation from Northern High School in Detroit, **Jo** moved in with my parents until I returned. They became life-long friends, and I'm sure they are together in heaven at this second. I want to be with them, this very second. They were wonderful people living a beautiful life while on earth and now enjoying heaven together.

I remember when **Jo** and my mother visited me at the military training facility on the campus of the University of Missouri. They both came because it would not have been proper in 1943 for a young girl to travel with out an escort on such a visit. Since I was attending the pilot training course, my time had to be accounted for. When I did get some time off between classes, I could see two of the most important people in the world to me. Dad was to visit me at a later date if he could, and he did.

*I have the pictures from part of that visit; Mother and **Jo** together was a beautiful sight. All the cadets who saw them told me how attractive they were. Close to the same height, **Jo** had a smaller frame but each was lovely in her own way; they took good care of what God had given them. **Jo** and my mother would go to the movies while I was in class, but we always had dinner together. They shared my time and made me feel very important. They came to the marches, assemblies, and were even allowed to see some of our outside training.*

*There were about 100 of us young men in the special training, most away from home for the first time. We were housed in the fraternity houses on campus, and the sorority houses were on every other lot. The single guys had a field day, but all I could think of was my beautiful **Jo**. Our fraternity house was on the edge of a splendid golf course. It made the war in Europe seem very distant.*

*Mother and **Jo** stayed a week and then had to return home to Detroit. It was very hard not to see my loved ones, but even more difficult to say good-bye. They made great sacrifices to come see me, because they were superb people who did marvelous things for others. I came home after 34 months in the service. I had seen them only about 20 days in that entire time, including the 10 days of furlough before going overseas.*

***Jo** and I kept in touch with well over 2,000 letters. I still have every one. I returned to marry **Jo** with full approval of my parents; they wanted **Jo** in the family forever and knew we would be very happy together. Only I know what they meant to me. For what my mother, dad, and **Jo** did for me, I could never give them enough love. I loved them all more than it is conceivable to say.*

During the war

What I looked for most of all
in every day was mail call
Always saying she was fine
Jo's letters were my lifeline
Keeping me informed with each letter
saying soon we'll be together
Planning a future for the two of us
she knew for sure without a fuss
In the little love letters from her each day
my wonderful Jo always knew what to say.

Sigma Phi Epsilon University of Missouri, Columbia

Stamina

Jo and I were born in the Roaring 20's. The Roaring 20's came to a halt and the depressing 30's took over. It took strong and determined people to weather what was ahead of them. I know very little about **Jo's** childhood. She wouldn't talk about difficult times, but the Depression must have had a severe effect on her family who were living in a small Pennsylvania coal-mining town at the time. Her father was killed in a boating accident when she was eleven, and her sister Irene was nine, but this was never talked about either. Her mother worked long, hard hours to support herself and her two girls, which meant there was very little leisure time for them to spend together.

Jo and Irene were both working part-time jobs, attending school, and church when I met them. **Jo** was a baby in the hands of hard times; the future would depend on her stamina. She looked forward to a challenge, if it was in the right direction and she was always up to the task.

The foundation for the future couldn't be built on solid ground. It meant rebuilding your life as you moved ahead and each time a new foundation was needed. I never knew much about **Jo's** early life or my own, just what was told to us by older family members. Her parents loved **Jo** very much, and I was loved very much by mine. When you put **Jo** and me together, our two loves had to mean happiness, contentment and pleasure. **Jo** and I knew that love had to be cultivated. When **Jo** did something for me or I did something for **Jo**, love would bloom. I call that cultivating at its best.

Each day was a pleasure to be around **Jo**. If you will plan ahead, think of the future, prepare for better things, keep a positive outlook, put your best foot forward, be loyal, honest, kind, hard-working, do more than your share, then you would have a prescription for what **Jo** accomplished. She had stamina from the hard start she endured and inspired me to do as she was doing. I could never attain the success or accomplish as much as **Jo**, but it was such a pleasure to be her husband and try.

When I ask you to **remember my Jo**, it's because then you'll always be remembering good things. **Jo's** smile was always showing in everything she did and the work she did was always in a positive direction. You know that only good things could happen in her plans. **Jo** loved to talk about our life together, always thinking good thoughts; happy with the life we were living. She was energetic and positive in everything she did. **Jo** would not bring up or linger over sorrow. She honored those who had gone before us in her prayers, by attending church services, and by visiting them at the cemetery, never forgetting them.

Jo learned from the start how to endure
hurting at a young age, that's for sure
Ups and downs she could take
often talking about her faith
When I stumbled I felt her hand
she would squeeze, it felt so grand
We held hands all through our life
touching would relieve our strife
So much comfort she would give
Jo made it a pleasure for me to live.

Jo and Ken Growing Up

Growing up during the Depression, **Jo** and I couldn't know that we were poor; we were too young. School was our first experience in the world outside our home. I had 10 cents for lunch money in grade school and that was considered being rich!

The first school I remember attending was Fairbanks. The biggest crime in this school was chewing gum or dipping a girl's pigtails in the inkwell. If you said a swear word you were taken to the principle's office, a nurse was called, and your mouth was washed out with soap. I knew it happened a couple of times, but never to me. If you caused trouble by starting fights, interrupting a class several times, or were a general troublemaker, you would be sent to a different school. I never knew of any one being sent away. Your parents knew of your standing in the school at all times, because the school called on them if you did anything wrong. It was a smart policy that worked for everyone's good.

I walked 12 city blocks to my next school, Hutchin's Intermediate. I was very thankful for the fine education that I received from remarkable teachers and a good administration. We had no guards, no locks, and no trouble; what we had was a lot of reading and homework. I remember being in the hospital for an emergency appendectomy and a teacher showed up with my school work. I was very happy, because I wouldn't be set back a half grade; I could stay with my class and friends. **Jo** was very happy about her education, too. She was a very good student and got excellent grades. I saw some of her schoolwork and it was perfect.

My father didn't have much of a chance for a good education, because he was an orphan. He went to night school on his own at *different times in his life, always trying to better himself. He did very well. He was the kind of person who wouldn't ask you to do something he wouldn't do. His handwriting was a thing of beauty and he was an excellent speller – much better than I.*

I never knew much about my mother's education. She was the oldest of five children, so she left school early to help in raising them. Mother did very well for us because she was a solid worker and had a phenomenal knowledge of life. Together Dad and Mother were a remarkable team, always making progress in whatever they attempted.

Dad gave financial help to a couple who were instrumental in raising him, Clara and Joe (Big Boy) Berger. They belonged to a church, worked a lot of farms for other people and had more loyal friends than anyone I ever knew. They had been very good to my dad when he was orphaned, so he felt he couldn't do enough for them. Dad loved and honored them very much. They meant a great deal to our family. Clara was a young schoolteacher when she lost almost all of her hearing, which ended her career. She still retained the knowledge, so she was able to do exceptional things with her life. Clara, I am sure, tutored my dad and always loved being a teacher. I called them "grandma" and "grandpa;" they were hard-working, church-going, wonderful people. When Joe Berger died, my parents took care of Clara for many years thereafter. They gave her anything she would accept, such as trips to visit us, but she liked her small town and friends back home. ***Jo*** *and I missed her very much when she passed. I don't have the words to tell you how marvelous the good people we knew were to* ***Jo*** *and I. We were blessed with knowing some wonderful, honest, kind, charming people, which is only the tip of the iceberg of our blessings.*

Neither ***Jo*** *nor I could believe the changes taking place in some of the schools today. Schools didn't teach us about drugs, guns, or sex. We* *didn't have to be taught not to steal, not to fight, and not to hurt; we learned these things at home. I knew love from my parents, my church, and my wonderful **Jo**. Most of the people I talk about didn't even have locks on their doors; they simply lived a good life.*

__Jo__ and I believed that profanity was the lack of vocabulary. No truly educated person can defend profanity. Profanity pollutes the environment, so always stay away from pollution. I'm very sorry that the airways are filled with smut, bad manners, and profanity under the excuse of freedom of speech. It is so dispirited and so demeaning.

Why do people have to hate?
violence Jo wouldn't tolerate
Love and kindness were first on our list
never raise your hand or your fist
A good education shows you the way
to enjoy this earth day after day
God gave us this earth to improve
leaving it up to me and you
Jo taught me what's right
and to do our share
If you "Remember My Jo,"
I know you'll care.

Mother Leta and Dad Alton

What I write about Leta and Alton is mostly second-hand, private reminiscences told to me by our relatives. Dad was 20 years old with a little money in the bank from his first job as a hotel maintenance boss in St. Louis, Missouri, when he heard that the automobile factories were hiring people to build cars in Detroit. He couldn't get there fast enough. He loved the challenge of it all and, being mechanically inclined, he had found the work he would enjoy doing for the rest of his life. He met and fell in love with Leta at first sight, just like **Jo** and me. Looking back and remembering what he told me, my love for **Jo** was a carbon copy of his love. I know my Mother was someone very special, bearing me at a young age and starting her own beauty shop at 17. Mother worked nearly 20 years, then sold her business to enable her to stay at home to take care of Dad, who was very ill at the time.

Most of my early family stories came from a couple of mother's sisters. They both felt Mom and Dad were the best people they had ever known. What I'm writing about now is how wonderful they were to their son. I knew from the age of about 10 that I had more than most, but my aunts said I had everything Mother and Dad could give me. I had a great deal of loving care – first child, everything new. I had music lessons, trips to Ohio, often staying for months at a time and camp; these were big things during the Depression. They had both had a very hard life and wanted their son to have as much as they could afford. They had big plans for my future college and then go into business with Dad. Dad

Mother's beauty shop in 1927

was disappointed when I couldn't go to college because of the advent of World War 11, but I was in pilot training at the University of Missouri. It was a special course and lasted for a few months. It wasn't what my Dad had planned for me, but he was with me in anything I did. He did get to see me fly a couple of times much later in my training and was very proud of my achievement.

Mother and Dad wanted a very special girl for the son they thought was special. ***Jo*** *said she hoped Mother and Dad would like her. I told her, "they will fall in love with you as I did." When I told Dad about* ***Jo*** *he was very upset that she wasn't of our religion. Mother said, "he*

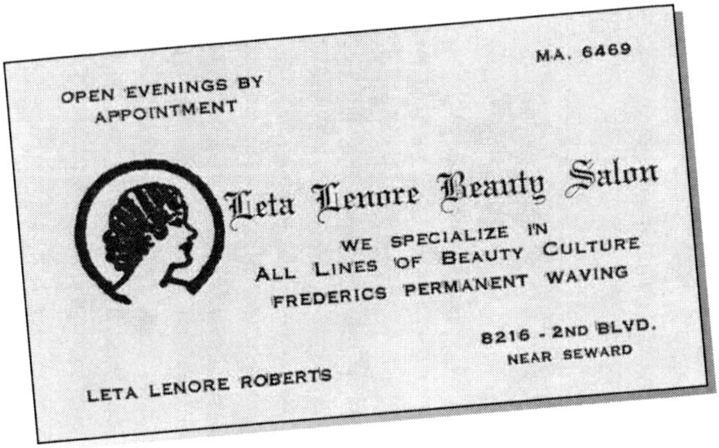

*will come to love **Jo**, but knowing him it will take a long time." But in a few months time we couldn't believe that **Jo** had won him over so completely. He couldn't do enough for her. Mother and Dad both asked me how I had managed to find this exquisite girl. They were both so happy with her and happy for us that we made plans to be married as soon as I returned from the service.*

*After the war, Mother, Dad, **Jo**, and I meshed perfectly and we couldn't do enough for each other. In the new house, we felt we had some time in Heaven. It was so wonderful. **Jo** was the catalyst; she was our queen bee. **Jo** could accept things so gracefully that you felt you had received much more than she and if it felt that way, you had. I had that feeling all our married life; each time I gave something to **Jo**, the gladness that came back to me was greater than the gift.*

*Repetition could go on forever, love repeated again and again that still would fall short of my praise of Mother, Dad, and **Jo**. I hope I've been able to tell you, with the help of my book and these few pictures, what a wonderful life I enjoyed for the short time I was here on earth.*

A young couple who improved
whatever they touched
always giving love, couldn't measure
how much
Leta and Alton, names seldom heard
bringing such joy into this world
Depression and war, feeling such pain
never looking for monetary gain
Jo and I were blessed by knowing
Mom and Dad
Their loving us were the best times we had
Leta and Alton, let's double date
being in heaven, it's never too late.

Skippy

We always had a dog; I never knew life without one. The first dog that was really mine was a little terrier puppy sent to me from Clara and (Big Boy) Joe when I was about four. They told Dad and Mom in a letter that they wanted me to have one of Trixie's pups. Trixy was a small terrier who was the constant companion for Clara. This little girl dog was a God – send to Clara. When the phone or the doorbell rang, or if some one were around, Trixy would let Clara know. Even though her hearing was bad, if you shouted into the phone, Clara could get the message.

When my Dad and Mom told me I was going to have my own puppy, I had a hundred questions – "When, what color, what would we name it?" We decided on the name Skippy.

Clara and Joe couldn't call on the phone as they didn't have extra money, but in the letter they said they would send Skippy as soon as they could. They had a lot of snow, but the first break in the weather and Skippy would be on his way. They would send Skippy by train and he would have to be picked up at the train station.

It was winter and we had a great deal of snow. It was very hard to get around, even in the city. Very few people traveled by car. The farmers had their cars on blocks, put away for the winter. Highway traffic was out of the question.

`Every night after work, Dad would bundle up in his very long winter coat and head for the train station, hoping to pick up Skippy. I didn't go, it was too cold out, and cars didn't have heaters yet. It was treacherous even for my dad. but would have been life-threatening for me. Each night when my dad returned – "no pup." The fourth night he looked very sad; he said "no pup", but the flap on his big coat pocket opened up and the head of Skippy looked out! The pocket started to quiver as Skippy wagged his little tail and I was the happiest little boy on this earth. We put him on the floor of my mother's shop and he raced all around, the happiest little pup I'd ever seen.

My Dad and Mother would tell this story to anyone who would ask or when anyone talked about dogs. When they told **Jo** this story many years later; she said she felt she knew how that little boy felt. Clara and Joe, too, always talked about sending the pup to us and how they enjoyed knowing that they were a part of such joy.

Jo and I had seven dogs in all. They got the best care and love from **Jo**. We were both retired when Charger, our last dog, died. We felt he was so exceptional that we couldn't replace him.

Picture of Jo

Jo has had that effect on me. I know that nothing could replace my **Jo**. I must be content with memories until I'm with my **Jo** again. I know I'll be as ecstatic as that little boy was and then some.

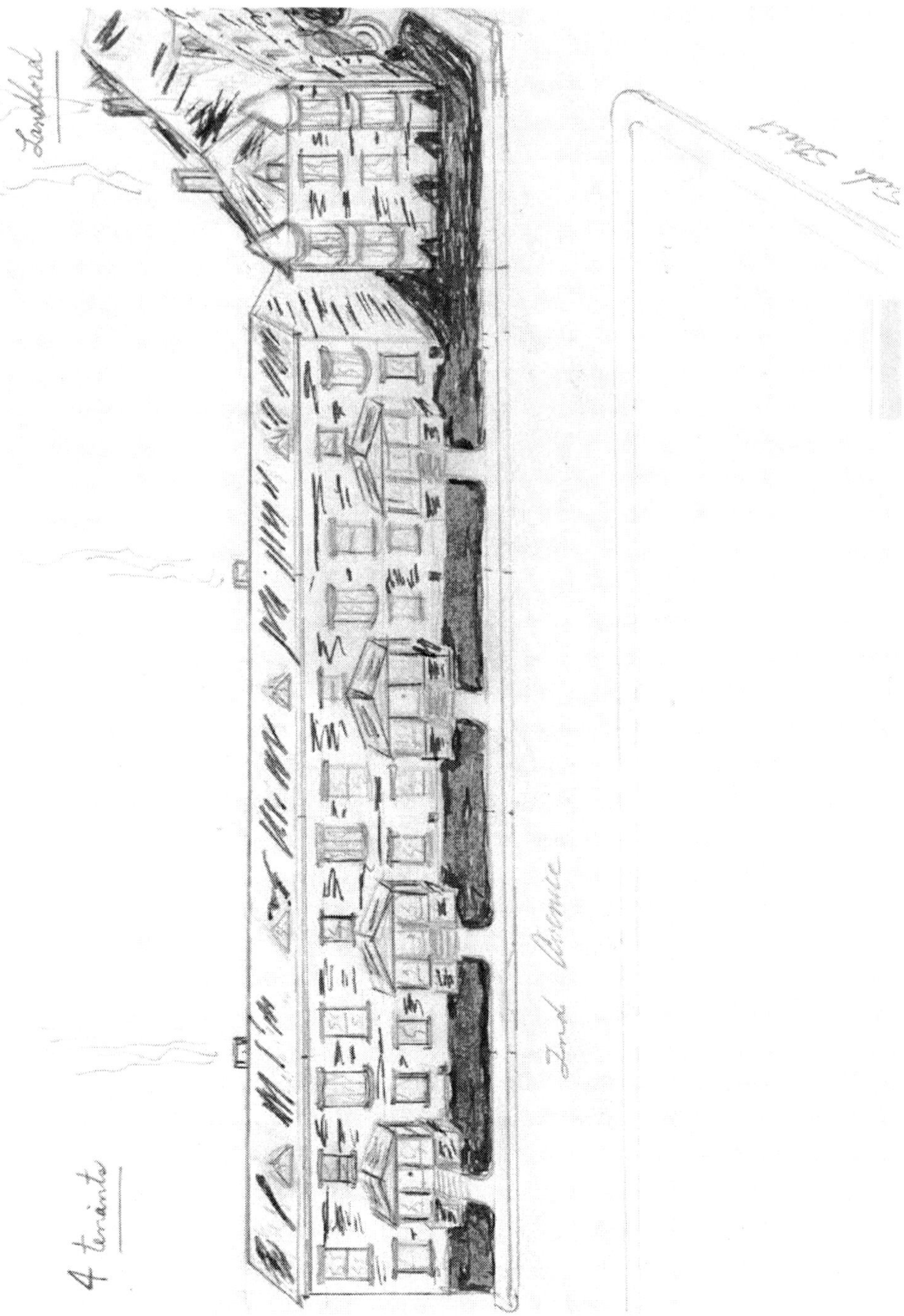
Landlord
4 tenants
2nd Avenue

Landlord

The house that my parents rented in Detroit in the late 1920's was built in the late 1800's. The first thing you saw was the landlord's home, a very large brick house with towers. It was very well-built and a real beauty in it's day. It was twice as large as the tenant's homes. Which had small front and back porches with very little lawn in front and back, the houses were connected side-by-side.

The years had treated this area well, even during the Depression. The General Motors Building, the Fisher Building and Ford Hospital were all within walking distance. There were many beautiful homes in the area, as well. I believe these homes were private dwellings originally, but hard times had turned them into business properties. Mother and Dad had picked a good location for her business. A bookstore was to our left, a laundry and grocery store were to our right. Across the street was a modern Church, a very attractive place of God.

The places have been torn down now, but the memories are still with me, even though this was over 65 years ago. Our original landlord sold out to the couple I call Mr. and Mrs. L. Mrs. L. would come into my mother's beauty shop once a week to get her hair done. They became good friends and spent a lot of time together. Seeing me one day, Mrs. L. asked if I could come over to play with her daughter, Mary, who was around 6 years old, just about my age. My mother was happy that I had a new playmate and was being chaperoned by Mrs. L. Mary had all the toys possible and I always looked forward to playing in " The Big Castle," the name we gave to the landlord's house. Mary and I would play tag and hide-and go-seek or we would color in our coloring books. We had a few other playmates, but not a lot; sometimes another girl or boy cousin of Mary's would join in our play.

Dad had to ask Mr. L's permission to paint Mother's shop; Mr. L. told him that was great and that he would supply the paint. Later, when Dad wanted a hopper to put the coal in the furnace, Mr. L. said, " order it. I'll pay for it, it's in the house I own." Mr. L. was a good landlord to our family. This home was so much nicer than the apartment we'd previously rented; so much more spacious. The big bay windows gave us a good view and ventilation. It was soundproof compared to the apartment and much more private. My mother, dad and I were always near. The big kitchen was wonderful and could seat company comfortably. Cooking was very important in those days and **Jo** always placed cooking high on her list, as did mother. With four big bedrooms, we could have relatives and friends live with us. There was an attic with an extra room, but it was too hot most of the summer. Still it provided plenty of extra storage space. Dad rented a nearby garage, so we wouldn't have trouble parking.

One day Mary and I were running around playing in "The Big Castle" when we entered a certain room and saw huge stacks of money on the table. A lot of big men were "playing," with the money. We saw that some of the men had badges on and some looked like they were going to a party, all dressed up in suits and ties. When I told my dad about what I had seen, he told me I had seen something I shouldn't and to forget it. I asked if it was bad. He answered that it was bad, but we couldn't call the police, because they were already there. It wasn't until I was much older that I understood what he was talking about – the men with badges were police and the ones in suits and ties were city officials. Mary and I saw those men come and go many times. We thought, in our childhood innocence, that it must have been a fun game that they were playing.

Mr. L's business was flowers and at Christmas time they sold a lot of Christmas trees, giving us the best he had. Whenever he saw us, he *would pick us up and play. We loved Mr. L. very much and looked forward to playing with him. He would chase us and hide from us; he was just a big, fun kid to us.*

Once I asked Mary if we could walk to school together, but she told me she went to a private school. I thought that meant family school just for her family since we didn't attend school together. We soon grew apart, only seeing one another by chance; still I have fond memories of how nice she was.

Many, many years later, I learned that Mrs. L. had told my mother that her husband had no money when he started selling flowers near the church across the street. He set up a stand on the 20-foot of property between the Castle and the tenant's homes, renting it from our original landlord. As a result of several wise investments, he was able to purchase "the Big Castle" and all the tenant's homes. We found out that those wise investments were putting some very strong, muscular men on his payroll – bodyguards and bouncers. I would take the rent over to his flower business once a month and give it to one of these huge men who were busily arranging flowers, when they weren't busy with some other job.

One summer Mary and her mother suddenly moved away. Before leaving, Mrs. L. had told my mother that Mr. L. had a new lady friend and wanted a divorce. Mr. L. had given her two choices, move to Grosse Pointe and raise Mary with a good-size allowance and while giving him all visitation rights or vanish. She chose to move to Grosse Pointe. Mother lost touch with her after that, but she heard from some of her regular clients that she and Mary were doing all right.

There was an enterprising young man who saw Mr. L's business prospering, running day and night. When you're delivering flowers in expensive specially built Packard trucks, it's sure to draw attention to your flourishing business. This young man decided to open a rival flower business within a half block of Mr. Landlord. Mr. Landlord, not wanting to share the profits with a newcomer, used his business savvy to put this new boy down the block out of business. You must remember that outlaws and gangsters were heroes to a lot of people in those days. Dad was from Missouri and told a lot of people about shaking hands with Frank James, the outlaw brother of an even bigger outlaw, Jesse James. Dad, always telling the truth, said he never met Jessie. Dad was proud to know Mr. L, too, and felt he was a very nice man. His views changed many years later when he heard more stories about how Mr. L. ran his business and his life. No one who knows a person who is real good to them wants to believe that they could be bad. When Mr. L. treated a bad element bad, you overlooked it. This still holds true with politicians, rock stars, athletes or any of our modern day cultural heroes.

Since Mr. L. owned the tenant's homes, he told the bookstore to move to a new location, because he had another use for their space. Connecting the basement of his flower business with the basement of the old bookstore via a tunnel, he put a new name on the new store, making everyone think competition had moved in even closer. He made it seem like there was another new flower shop right next to his original shop. Mr. L's plan was to cut prices by placing big signs out front showing that a price war had broken out.

The buying public rushed to these two stores to take advantage of the situation. The prices had gotten so low that people were lining up to buy inexpensive flowers; at one point he was giving away some orchid corsages. The new man on the next block couldn't compete for long and was soon forced to close his doors. Mr. L. took the signs off the new store then as if they, too, had gone out of business.

He had taken a potential threat and used it to come up with a huge plus, as well as gaining more office space and refrigeration for his original flower shop. Mr. L. was a good businessman and his flower business grew as well as his name; he eventually became very well known all over the world. When I told ***Jo*** *about Mr. L, whom she knew, it was hard for her to believe his lifestyle. We hoped Mary had a good life.* ***Jo*** *only wanted good things; remember she was my angel.*

Big Boy and Clara

Clara and Joe Berger raised my father for a few years when he was a boy, even going so far as applying for permission to adopt him. Clara and Joe worked farms for other farm owners and lived in the big farmhouses, so I thought they owned them. I thought they were rich. In reality, they were poor, but hard working, loving people.

My mother's beauty shop was a six-day operation. We lived in an apartment, so it was best for me to go to Ohio during the summer and stay with Joe, "Big Boy" as I called him, and Clara. I was a very small boy when I took my first summer vacation with them. Mother and Dad knew that this arrangement was a win-win situation. This would be good for me and they would pay a generous amount to Clara and Big Boy for my care even though Clara and Big Boy always felt it was not necessary. When you're young and growing, a change of life style is a good learning experience. I would attend church, visit large farm families, and be around farm animals. My father knew how Clara and Joe had raised him and wanted that for me. I would learn a lot from wonderful people, just like he had.

One year I asked my parents to let me stay with the Bergers throughout the school year and they agreed. It was a lot different from the city. Riding a school bus gave me time and opportunity to learn how farmers and their families lived. So did going into the small nearby town on Saturday night to talk about everything that had happened that week, about the animals and the work that had been done, all the new births and what the future might hold for us all. It was a totally new world to me. We would talk to neighbors gathered in the street, women in-groups and the men the same all over town. The children would be rushing around, playing tag and any other games they could devise. We would visit the ice cream factory on the edge of town and then head for home, Clara telling Joe what news she had found out and Big Boy doing the same. It was always a productive and joyous occasion. What a wonderful way that was to live.

The summer I turned 12 Big Boy was roofing a barn at a racetrack and got me a ride on a racehorse. Big Boy was a jovial prankster, who looked and played the part. I loved him, because he put some love and speed in my life, and he had so much love for his dear wife Clara. She had lost her hearing, so he would use that opening to tell me in secret how he adored her. If she by chance heard him, she would take out after him, two elderly grown-ups acting like children, making their love even stronger. Clara and Joe were always together and always looking out for the welfare of others.

If possible every Friday late in the day, Clara and Joe would go fishing. They were welcome at the many streams and fishing holes of their farmer friends. Anyone who knew Joe and Clara always welcomed them with open arms. Big Boy would find out from his friends through the week where the fish were biting, and then he would tell Clara. The joy they would get in planning this fishing trip was always a pleasure for me to witness. Joe would get in the car early on that Friday and say, "Clara will get in the car and as soon as we move twenty feet, she'll shout, "stop the car; I forgot something." It was always true. It tickled me that he knew her every thought and move. Joe would tell Clara that she was breaking too many branches or stepping on too many twigs, then say to me as an aside, " The fish won't bite; she's making so much noise, this trip will be a waste." We always caught a lot of fish, then Joe would tell everybody he encountered of Clara's great catch, giving her all the credit. I call that loving your partner.

I was with them in one of the coldest of winters when they were living in a huge farmhouse. All of the upstairs bedrooms with fireplaces were not being used. The kitchen was very large and contained a big wood-fired iron stove that we warmed our bath water on. It was the only room that was heated. Clara cooked on this stove that was kept going at all times. Clara was so dignified and took such pride in her canning and cooking ability. The canning she prepared for you was a gift from heaven.

Our sole entertainment at night was to play several games of rummy. If you got a run of three or four of the same cards you could lay them down. If you laid all your cards down at once, the game was over and you had won. Because Clara couldn't hear him, Big Boy would shield his lips and whisper to me what cards he needed. Clara knew what he was doing and would shout at him as we played the game. The three of us would have such fun. She would bawl him out and he would deny it. This would tickle me – all little boys like good-natured trickery. Clara had as much fun with her part of the act as we did. Then Joe would say, "last game," as our evening together drew to a close.

When the last game was over, Big Boy and I would make a mad dash for our beds. If you got in bed first, you would holler out, "I won!" This was the big prize of the night. We would discard our shoes, pants, and shirts on the way to bed. Clara would later pick up our discards and lay them out for us. It was part of the game, but she would still tell us how bad we were. When the last game started, Big Boy would drop a card, reach down and untie his shoe, then cover it up with his pant leg. He would silently undo his overalls – he was getting a head start while I would be doing the same thing. Undressing in secret, but both knowing it at the same time. That's what made it so much fun!

During a bad winter day when I was stuck in the house, I practiced undressing, running up the stairs, running down the hall, and leaping for the bed. "I'll win tonight," I think, "as I have practiced all the tricks and my leap in bed. I can get my shoes, shirt and pants off as I rapidly ascend the stairs, run down the hall, and take my giant leap. Grandpa won't believe how fast I can move. This will be my Gold Medal performance in the Olympics."

That night Big Boy announced, "last game," and the race was started in secret. Clara won, laying down all her cards. I got off to a good start – my practice had paid off. I rushed into my room, made my famous leap, and you guessed it – ***The Bed Was Gone****! I fell forever, searching for the bottom, ending up on feathered pillows and a soft comforter – but it wasn't my bed! Big Boy had stayed back earlier to bring a light and that must have been when he had prepared this* *surprise for me. Clara couldn't believe what she was seeing. Big Boy enjoyed the startled look and the rumbled heap I was in. He had assured Clara that I couldn't get hurt, because of the way he had cushioned the floor and wall. It was a softer landing than usual. The next day I joined in the laughter about our race to bed. Big Boy's words of wisdom were, "Look before you leap!" The way Big Boy told the story was fun for everybody. He praised my speed, my undressing, and my moving in the dark. He even told it as if I had been the winner. I'd heard Big Boy tell that story for years. It was all in fun and a joy I've never forgotten.*

Clara and Big Boy, a jovial pair
having such fun when we got there
Callused hands from turning the ground
such a pleasure to be around
Always working, knowing success
Clara so happy with her new dress
Sure to thank God at each meal
playing the hand that he did deal
In simple things, they found such pleasure
loving each other was forever their treasure.

When I was six or seven years old, Joe and Clara let me stay with Clara's sister's family the Dewey's. Big Boy, being the prankster he was, started telling me scary stories about their house; Clara told him to stop, but Big Boy continued out of range of Clara's hearing. "Wait till you see," he said, "the house is haunted by ghosts, but I'll protect you." I asked, "who haunts the house?" "Nobody knows," he said, "it could

be anyone from the past." If you stay very quite at night, you'll hear them walking about, the steps creaking and even chains rattling." It upset Clara for him to talk about the haunted house. My **Jo**, *like Clara, didn't like scary things either.*

It was on a Friday night when we first approached the house. It sat a half of a mile down a lane that ran parallel to a single railroad track. We had to slow down on the muddy road, then speed up to climb the steep mound in the road built up with gravel and rocks for the railroad tracks, make a sharp left turn, then go down a steep grade to enter the lane. Big Boy had to stop the sputtering old Ford, and get out to open the gate, hoping all the while that the four cylinders would keep running. Opening the car door let all the fury of the storm wildly flash on us. Grandma wrapped herself around me as if to shield me from the sheets of rain, wind, lightning and thunderclaps. It was an awesome power for Big Boy to have his way with, the storm's fury forcing him in different directions. Grandpa struggled with the car door, hanging onto parts of the car and fence to keep from slipping and sliding into the oozy mud. He was soaked from head to foot and we still had a long way to go.

He returned to his chugging car and moved it past the gate; not wanting any animals to be able to get out the next morning. Lighting and thunder crashed around the sky and earth. The fences along the tracks had bushes and vines that were moving in the strong winds generated by the storm. The old Ford, as if knowing something was wrong, didn't seem to want to move; fearing what was still ahead, it was slowly chugging along. We felt it wanted to give up, to me this was not a good sign. I was sitting between Big Boy and Clara in the front seat. Grandpa was wet to the bone. and at that time there were no heaters in cars, unless you were very rich. The old worn-out hand-

operated wiper blades on the windshield didn't afford us a good view, but what I saw I didn't like. The headlights in those days didn't shine even two car lengths, so in a storm, or even a light rain, you parked or stayed home. As we slowly approached the house, we could see oil lamps were flickering throughout, casting huge mysterious, menacing shadows. If Big Boy hadn't told me this place was haunted, I would have guessed it on my own. I was very frightened and we hadn't even arrived yet, but I wouldn't let anyone know how afraid I really felt.

A big man holding a lantern greeted us at his back door. He assured us that his house was a shelter from this horrifying storm, the worst he'd seen in some time. He was happy to see us arrive safe and sound. This man and his wife had five boys and five girls, the youngest child being only a couple years older than myself. Clara had told me before we left the farm, "you're going to love these children." When we entered the great room that they were all gathered in, I found to my delight that I was a new toy for them to play with. They focused so much attention on me; I couldn't help but have a wonderful time. They passed me around and I was hugged and kissed until I could scarcely catch my breath.

The only board game they had to play was a four-in-one-game. It was a wooden board on which you played checkers or shot the little wooden rings into pockets. They were very careful with this toy, because it was the only one they possessed. Soon I forgot all about the storm raging around us and the idea that this was a haunted house. The children and I had nothing but fun that night.

In the morning, they couldn't wait to show me what animals they had, each child wanting me to see something special of his or her own. They shared with me what they knew about living on a farm and farming. I learned that farmers worked very hard and that their children pitched in to do a lot for the parents they honored. Zeppy, a horse who had been put out to pasture after being retired from plowing, was the one the children rode. She would lumber along, carrying each one of us in turn, happy for the attention.

The Dewey farm was very large and a lot of hard work was required to utilize it productively. They had no mechanized equipment of any kind and no electricity, so they had no electrical motors. Consequently, they used only hand-cranked equipment to shell corn, sharpen tools, and pump water. The shelled corn went to feed a couple hundred chickens, some turkeys, geese, even some guineas and other fowl. You could work from sunup to sundown on most family farms and always have much more to do. Living on a working farm that could support an entire family was a wonderful way of life – waking up each morning, working together all day and always loving one another. The family attended church together, too, always praying for better things, believing God wanted better things for everyone. Staying with them that weekend created a lot of memories that I cherish to this day.

A few years later, I stayed with this family for nine days. Big Boy was right all those years ago about there being a ghost of some kind in that house. I heard someone on the steps, heard strange noises, heard strange voices, but with over fifteen people in the house, who needed ghosts? The family took food and water upstairs, but it was all hush, hush. Someone they wouldn't talk about lived on the fourth floor, in the attic. Whoever was up there never came down while I was there. I believe it was kept secret from the younger children, also. In those days, people seldom talked about family matters that might be considered a hardship. They were such a nice family that I know they did the best they could for everyone. Many years later, I heard that Mr. Dewey carelessly crossed a field one-day in which he had pastured a prize bull; he should have known better. He was badly mauled when the bull attacked. He remained crippled for the rest of his life, but his children took good care of him, keeping the family love alive.

Jo and I drove around that part of the country many years later, looking for the haunted house I had told her about. It was so vivid in my mind that I was sure if we found it, she would understand how scary it was to a little boy. Maybe it was the age that I saw it that made it so strongly imprinted in my mind. I had seen haunted houses in books, but believe me, this was classic plus. Things had changed so much we never found what we were looking for, but I remembered that I was never afraid of the house once I was in it. The loving people who lived there never let fear enter. They made their guests feel at home.

A haunted house is terror enough
a fear no one should ever trust
Inside me I shouted can't we wait
seeing it from that far off gate
Lightning and thunder abounds all around
old car slipping, sliding on muddy ground
Lanterns flickering in a ghostly light
my heart pounding from the fright
A wonderful family took that away
the sun came up for a beautiful day

I told **Jo** about the fun Joe and Clara had been and she laughed at all my stories. We looked forward to visiting them and planned a trip. I told **Jo** what a great storyteller Big Boy was and the fun we were *going to have. I knew that Big Boy had been hurt from a fall, but I thought he was back to his good old self. We arrived only to find that he would never be the Big Boy I had known as a youth. The joy was gone out of his life; he looked good, but he couldn't participate. I have arrived at that point in my life now; without* ***Jo****, I can't participate. I hope that* ***Jo*** *and I can see Big Boy and Clara, run into the small town on a Saturday night, meet all the good people we ever knew, and find that joy we missed in life. Small towns always loved my* ***Jo****.*

I think ***Jo*** *and I would have liked farm life, the people and the calmness. We did live a somewhat country life. Franklin, within walking distance of our home, was the town that time forgot. It's an historic town still hanging on to some of the original buildings. Time is changing it now, but* ***Jo*** *and I did enjoy over thirty years of seeing it almost everyday. For the first ten years we lived nearby horses trotted down the Main Street, but they are gone now.*

I believe we were successful in our lives because of ***Jo*** *and her planning.* ***Jo*** *always thought of others. She always wanted to share with our families; trying to keep us together in all her plans. Then things began to change. People stopped planning. Something began to happen with most of the people. The "me" generation moved in, everything now being done not for "the family," but for "me."*

Many years ago, houses had no locks on the doors. Most farmhouses had guineas that roosted in a tree near the house. It was to let you know that something was wrong – a fire or a stranger needing help. If any stranger approached during the night, the guineas would screech. They were our first home alarms, letting us know that someone needed help. In the world today alarms are on everything, telling you that trust and common decency is almost gone. There are guards everywhere you go, even in the shopping malls. My cars and my home are alarmed. I've even heard that city officials took the fire alarms off the street corners, because people were stealing them. I'm sure God doesn't approve of the things that are happening to this wonderful country and he is displeased with those who break the commandments.

Clara and Joe, good people to the end, had a 50th wedding anniversary; **Jo** and I were able to celebrate ours, too. Dad and Mother had theirs in heaven. Won't it be wonderful when we have our 100th in heaven, all of us together again? I'm sure God has planned that for us.

If we could bottle all the good that was
in Jo
giving it to everyone so they could know
How wonderful it is to spread love around
it would work in big cities as well as small
town's
The joy I received from Jo was inconceivable
the love she gave me was unbelievable
Jo had so much fun by just being nice
proving that girls are sugar and spice
Seeing her sharing, Jo always giving more
spreading love and joy knowing all would adore
Jo tried every day to make the world a better
place
I know she succeeded in her loving, caring space

Thanksgiving

Times have changed a lot, but in the late twenties if you had enough money to buy a turkey, you could be called rich. Mother and Dad weren't rich, but Dad won two turkeys at the Chrysler Gun Club where he was Secretary. It took some good shooting to win the contest, but Dad had talent. He learned to shoot on the family farm where shooting game birds put food on the table.

Mother was a very hard working young woman, operating her beauty shop six days a week. Running the shop was hard physical work for her, plus having to stand on her feet all day. In addition, she was dealing with the public, ordering supplies, and making sure the money to pay for them was there when it was due. The beauty shop was close to a major hospital, so the clientele consisted mainly of nurses. It is a well-documented fact that hospitals have more work during hard times, so this helped keep Mother working, but times were so bad that it hurt everyone; any extra money Dad or Mother made went to help out their families. I loved my Dad and Mother so much, and at my tender age, I already knew they could do anything.

Mother was at the shop every day. Every penny counted, so she had to be there just in case there were some walk-in customers. Mother's shop wasn't fully established yet, so if business was slow she would work on friends and family for free. "Finger waves," she'd say, " use very little product." It kept her busy, made a lot of friends and relatives happy, and made the dark days a little brighter. Mother's entire family – her sisters, brother and parents – lived on the other side of town, so we didn't see them often unless they dropped by the shop during the day.

My parents wouldn't let other's know, but they were supporting a lot of people. The windows didn't need to be washed, but Mom would *have it done by an Uncle who wouldn't take money unless he earned it. That type of thing was going on all the time. You couldn't let your family or friends starve. Dad's brothers were scattered, mostly in farm country, so he felt they would be all right. Dad had a beautiful handwriting ability and he tried to keep in touch with them through letter writing, but most of them never wrote back.*

When my Dad won the first turkey, he was told to pick it up at a poultry slaughterhouse. This was no supermarket, factory-cleaned, frozen bird; all the feather-plucking and preparing was done by the consumer. I clearly remember having to have scalding hot water to loosen the bird's feathers, pulling out all the big feathers, then pulling out the pin feathers with pliers or tweezers, and setting a newspaper on fire to singe the bird to burn all the hair off. Next you had to remove the internals, and then you had to cut off the feet. Some people made soup out of the less desirable parts, but some gave them away. I'm sure I missed a lot of things that had to be done, but believe me, I saw more than enough.

When Dad won the second turkey, Mom and Dad agreed to give it to Mother's family. Grandpa, a streetcar conductor, had been out of work a long time. No one had jobs to ride the streetcar to, so the city had cut back on service and he lost his job. Six mouths to feed, no money coming in, no new jobs to be had anywhere. Mother had planned on having them over for Thanksgiving, but that involved them getting on one of the few streetcars still running, dealing with transfers, and being out in the winter weather. Besides, our apartment was really too small for so many visitors. Now all the problems were solved. They could have their own turkey and we would have ours at home and then drop by after dinner to see them. We had a car and, weather permitting, we could visit with some other friends on the trip across town. This was shaping up be such a nice Thanksgiving Holiday.

The holiday was always a lot of work for the women. Still they looked forward to the great meal they would prepare for the family. It took advanced planning, money, and a lot of cooperation from both family and friends to do it right. There were no push-button stoves, no roasters either, so it took several hours to prepare a turkey. Help wasn't near by and there was no refrigeration, so you had to prepare the turkey before it spoiled. Only the rich had iceboxes. We didn't know anyone who had one. Ice had to be delivered; if you picked it up yourself, it was melted before you got home. Ice took most of the space in an icebox. You had a drip pan that had to be emptied as the ice melted. In our neighborhood, a lot of people had a window box that they had made themselves. It was a wooden box covered with tin that you hung outside your kitchen window; that day's weather was your temperature control. Open your window, open the box, put in or take out what you wanted to keep cold and hope it didn't freeze or spoil on you. A lot of progress had been made from the early pioneer days when they cooked outside with no water, so at least Mother did have a warm kitchen, a good stove, and hot and cold running water.

Mother got word to her family that thanks to Dad's marksmanship they could have their own turkey. They sent Johnny, her younger brother, to pick up the bird. When Johnny stopped by the beauty shop, Mother was so busy that she sent him to our apartment on his own with strict instructions on which turkey to take to Grandma and Grandpa. You guessed it; Johnny took the wrong bird. Mother and Dad got home late that night and discovered what had happened – the turkey they had worked so hard to prepare was gone. They almost collapsed, but picked themselves up and started preparing the second bird, happy to have one. They never said a word to my Mother's family for quite some time and I'm not sure who first told the story, but the moral was that a grand Thanksgiving was had by all.

*Many years later when I told **Jo** this story, she said, " knowing Leta and Alton, they would have it no other way. They would always choose to amend a mistake on their own." **Jo** loved Mother and Dad so much and they felt the same about her. I had the best parents on this earth and the finest wife. I give thanks everyday for my amazing life.*

Blanche

Blanche was a beautiful young woman who was in and out of my life for many years. Before she came to live with my parents and me, she had been married to a handsome young man. They had a little girl and were so happy with the future they felt they would have together. They were both very religious and so much in love, but it all came to a tragic end. At work one day, a hold-up man confronted him. It was his habit to put the bible he always carried with him under his arm when leaving his truck. The hold-up man said, "Hands up!" and the Bible dropped. As he reached for it, the hold – up man shot him dead. The local newspaper verified this account in the next morning's edition.

Blanche, now a young widow with a small child to support, received a large sum of money from the company he worked for and began to move on with her life. However a short time later she was in an auto accident and her foot was badly injured and burned. To save her foot, a metal pin was put in; it was the best the doctors could do at the time. Being unable to get around very well, she gained weight that added to the problem. Walking a city block with her twisted foot was almost impossible for her to endure. Inevitably, she was unable to have her baby with her and she sent her to live with an aunt in New York. How it must have hurt her to lose both her husband and their child.

Blanche became a seamstress and made her living working for friends and relatives; that is how she came to be living with us. We had very large rooms in our old house; the room my parents chose was ideal for Blanche. It had a bay window, so she could get plenty of light and view the street and church nearby. My dad made it into a bedroom and sewing room combined. Baseball was Blanche's great love; radio was most of her entertainment. She could sew while listening to her favorite pastime. The bathroom was also near. Blanche felt so blessed with this arrangement.

I was seven years old and became a constant companion of hers. My mother was busy in her beauty shop downstairs, so it was a boon to her for me to have a wonderful lady to share my time with. I would rush home from school and find both my mother and Blanche waiting for me in the same house. They would both help me with my schooling and give me work to keep me busy.

Blanche took me to a ball game once. Maybe you saw us – a lady limping along in pain, with a little boy hanging on, so proud of this wonderful lady. If you saw us that day I'm sure you will remember that Hank Greenberg hit a dozen balls out of the park that day at practice, but he didn't get a home run during the game.

That year I won an award for being the best safety patrol captain at Fairbanks School. The award was mostly for attendance and cleanliness. My mother made sure my clothes and white safety belts looked like new. The prize was said to be a trip to New York City, Niagara Falls, and places I had only dreamed of.

Blanche would pray for things to happen and she felt she could predict the future with God's help. She said I would go on this trip; she had prayed for it and God would not let her down. Many more schools entered, so a drawing was needed to select the winners. They had the drawing; I wasn't picked. I felt bad for some time, but Blanche would cheer me up by saying, "God has a better plan for you." She had a beautiful heart and soul.

Chrysler Corporation who had supplied the army trucks, tents and gear, decided the following year, that they would give the employees' sons a chance to take the same trip. You guessed it! My dad was an employee who qualified and I made that trip. It was terrific. I was a year older and could enjoy the trip even more. Blanche thanked God and was as happy as me knowing God had granted her wish.

Blanche seldom came downstairs during the day; it was too hard on her. One summer day she appeared ready to leave the house, so mother asked her where she was going. Blanche said she needed to get some things at the store. Mother told her we would help if she would only wait, but she felt she could do it herself.

It was very hot, no air conditioning, and a long block to walk. She then needed to get on the streetcar and ride five blocks to the dime store. Off and on, she required help to assist her, a real task with that twisted foot. When you saw the way she had to walk, it almost broke your heart. You could see the effort she had to make to be able to move at all. Mother worried about her all the time she was gone. When she returned, she was perspiring heavily, but in good spirits.

Home only a few minutes, she started out again. My mother rushed to her and asked what she was doing. "I've got to go back now," she said, "I had a package of buttons stuck to my sweaty arm." "Ken will be home in a few minutes," my Mother said, "he will take them back." Blanche replied, "It's my obligation. I need to take them back." She took them right back, asked for the manager, and told him what happened and that she was so sorry. She said God would want her to do the right thing and this was the right thing.

I was overseas when ***Jo*** *wrote of meeting Blanche and how they were both now living in our house, the lady who had helped raise me and the girl I would soon marry.* ***Jo*** *wrote me of the amazing clothes that Blanche made for her and the friendship they shared. Blanche made* ***Jo*** *a very special hostess coat, so much love was put into it's making. They talked for hours every chance they got. She called* ***Jo*** *"Dollie." Unfortunately,* ***Jo*** *and I never got to see Blanche together since she went to live with her daughter in New York City before I returned home from the war.*

You will read later about the wedding in Philadelphia. When we left that wedding, we went to New York looking for Blanche Smith. We tried, but to find a specific Smith in New York City was a losing proposition. We never found her. I believe she was still making people exstatic with the joy she always gave. Her work was remarkable and each person who knew her was enriched. She once wrote a note on a Christmas card that God had given her me to be with when she couldn't be with her daughter. God works in mysterious ways for those who believe. Blanche and **Jo** are in Heaven now. We couldn't find Blanche in New York, but I know **Jo** and I will find her in Heaven. We both loved Blanche very much.

Meeting Blanche all were
blessed
wanting to help so she could rest
Her desire was to please our Lord
silent, proud, but never bored
So much love with Blanche around
we were sure she was heaven bound
She told mother Ken replaced her child
knowing it was for only a little while
God works in mysterious ways
all of us at times count the days

Helen and Charley

Helen and Charley Dohring were my parent's best friends. The life they had was up and down in the early years. I want to say they are the ones who introduced us to Blanche. Helen was so soft and gentle, a lover of all things, while Charley was a loud man; his voice was very strong and, as children, my friends and I feared him. Once we got used to the strong voice we all liked him.

Dohring Family

Charley was a very talented carpenter. In the early 1920's he started his own business as a contractor. He was, also, a surveyor, but Charley was spread too thin, as most people were, when the depression hit. He lost everything, but his talent. His dream of making it big as an independent contractor was gone. Around Christmas time Charley would get the most beautiful Christmas tree and put real candles on it. They had a special holder – dangerous, but beautiful. They had a large family and lots of people would gather at the Dohring home. They always included us as members of their family. The men played pinochle for hours; it was a very serious game for them. The younger boys could watch the men play, but were never allowed to say a word; you could watch and learn, one word and you were gone. We couldn't ask questions, we had to learn by watching. It was our hope that we could set in for one of the men someday. It was usually your father who would let you set in for him, while he excused himself for a few minutes. On the way home I would ask my dad questions. "If you don't follow suit," I said, "what happens? Why didn't you play the ace of clubs that time and take the trick with the ten?" Once we got home Dad would deal four hands and show me how to bid and how to play. The day I was my father's partner in a real grown-up game was the highlight of that year; I must have been 15, but felt like a real man.

Dad and Charley worked on inventions together, always thinking ahead, mostly about gadgets for cars. They had a couple they tried out that really worked, but they never put them on the market. In his later years Charley worked as a carpenter and worked his way up to remodeling the presidential suite for the Book Cadillac, a very prestigious Detroit hotel. He was still surveying property to supplement his income, a real go-getter, when he fell and broke his hip. He was advised by his doctor to move to Florida; this was in the early forties. He lived in Florida the rest of his life, saying, "in Michigan I worked all summer and winter to get warm clothes and coal for that winter, but in Florida I don't need either." The Dohring's were a great asset to any place they lived. In Florida he would purchase a home, add beautiful rooms, sell it and start over again. He became well to do in his later years through home remodeling and land speculation.

From time to time they would come to Detroit to visit their sons, see other friends and purchase a new car. You could see it being built and then drive it home; it was a big savings in those days. When they met **Jo**, they fell in love with her and she with them. Charley always called my mother, " Big Red;" Mom had reddish hair, but I never understood the big part. Maybe it was because he called **Jo**, " Little **Jo**." "Big Red" and "Little **Jo**" loved Helen and Charley very much, but never had enough time with them on earth. I am sure it's different now.

Marcus of Hope College

When I was a teenager, the church I attended was Westminster Presbyterian, near Boston and Chicago Boulevards, a very rich area. The church elders were looking for a new leader for the Young People's Department and Hope College was one of the places they were recruiting. When Mr. Marcus, an award-winning athlete at Hope College, showed up with his new bride, all of us took notice. He was to be our baseball and basketball coach and Young People's instructor.

I was to see and learn things because of Mr. Marcus that I only imagined up till then. He was a great athlete, very handsome, friendly, and very well-liked in a short period of time. George Davis and another friend of mine got a job for the summer at Hope College; they came back telling us of the trophies Mr. Marcus had won and how he was still revered there.

I was dating **Jo**, working at the training school, helping my dad at his business and preparing for the Air Force. When you are young you can go day and night, the demand for your time is constant; you don't turn down anything and keep looking for more. I told **Jo** about Mr. Marcus and she got to see him as our coach at a basketball game. Our Young People's attendance doubled with Mr. Marcus and his wife joining our church; they were fine people you could look up to.

Some members of the church would invite him and his wife to stay in their homes while they were on vacation. Marcus would get permission to occasionally take a small group of Young People from the church into these homes. He wanted us to see what could be accomplished with hard work, a good education, and being religious. He told us how some of these people had started out in life as financially poor people. We saw inside-swimming pools, sauna, billiard room, and sunroom, exercise room, paintings of great value and even a bowling alley in one of these mansion-like houses. He hoped we would work hard and some day have some of the wonderful things this earth has to share.

One day during a basketball game, a member of our adult team was injured. He was accidentally bumped, injured his back when he fell, and was taken to the hospital. He could not work for a time and he needed money to help his family out; the church started collecting for his assistance. Mr. Marcus was keeping the money in a locked cabinet, but one night someone broke in and stole it. Marcus was being tested to become an FBI agent, so he got some of his friends with the Bureau to assist in the investigation. They found the two young boys who had taken the money. Their parents paid the money back, but the boys had to make restitution and then some. They said were sorry and would never do anything like that again. The man who was injured got well and went back to work shortly thereafter.

Many years later I heard that Mr. Marcus flew over 25 missions over Germany in World War 11, coming home a war hero, but in a relatively short time, killed himself. I hope that wasn't true. I remember what wonderful role models he and his wife had been. I never visited Hope College, but I understand he was a legend there forever. I didn't follow up on this story because I want to remember only good things and not look for the unthinkable. When I meet my **Jo** in heaven, we will be sure to look up Mr. Marcus, our hero from Hope College, and his wonderful wife.

Jewelry for Jo

Jo had her part-time job at the Conery, was my girlfriend now, and Christmas was rushing upon us. I asked her what she wanted and she said, "you don't have to get me anything," the same answer I would get for the next 55 years. "Please, **Jo**," I said, "you must want something special." "Ken," she replied, "I can't think of anything."

I talked to my Mother who knew **Jo** by now and liked her very much. We were going to the show a lot and I saw a gift book for **Jo's** sister, Irene. I asked Mother why I could find something for Irene and not **Jo**; she told me, "you're in love with **Jo**, that's why!" She told me she and Dad would be looking. "We want to get **Jo** something, too," she said, "we love her so much, Ken."

One day, not long after this conversation, Mother told me to get **Jo** a good watch; she pointed out how a watch is looked at all day long, is the first thing a girl puts on in the morning, and the last thing she takes off at night. "You enjoy it all day, while remembering who gave it to you. I'm sure **Jo** would like a watch from you," she said, adding, "if you're short money, I'll help you." We didn't know a jeweler, so it was window shopping for me. I found a small shop that had the watch I wanted in the window. I asked if it was guaranteed and was told, "for one year," so I bought it. Mother said it was very nice, sure that **Jo** would like it. She wrapped it up special so it was a present fit for a Princess, packaged with love. When I gave it to **Jo**, she was thrilled and so appreciative. Her being so happy made it a wonderful Christmas for me.

We were seeing each other everyday and I saw that she was proud of her new watch. One day when she didn't wear it, I asked her why; she said, "the clasp is broken." I told her I would take it back and get her a new one; I did, seeing the same man who sold it to me. He said, "the watch was guaranteed, not the clasp." He refused to repair or replace it. I could tell he was the bully type. He just walked away from me, giving me no satisfaction.

I was steaming, wanting to break something, smash something. "What's going on," I thought, "this is not a cheap watch." I decided that I would not tell anyone about this, I would take care of it myself. My dad had always told me, "Ken, when you have a problem, count to 10 and don't make things worse; take your time and work it out with a good solution. I know you can do it, you're my son." I went to another jeweler, who looked at it with the special glass; he felt it was cracked in the making, told me who manufactured it, and said he was sure I could get it replaced. He advised me to go back to the shop where I had originally purchased it. I knew that bully wouldn't give in, but suddenly I had the solution.

One of our neighbors had eight children, all friends of mine, who would do anything I asked. They had unlimited phone calls, so I made up a cardboard with the phone number of the jewelry store in big numbers. I remembered that he was in the store by himself, a one-man operation, and that the phone was in the back room where he worked.

I told my little friends to "call that number several times day and night and hang up, don't answer, when he picks up, just hang up." In a couple of days, I returned to the store and asked if he would fix the watch or did he want to keep on answering the phone? "You're costing me a lot of money," he angrily said. He took the watch and returned with a new one with a much better clasp. "Thank you," I said politely, as I turned and walked away smiling.

Dad deserves the credit for the instructions he gave me many years before, but ***Jo*** *was my motivation. I couldn't live with myself if I hadn't kept my promise to my girlfriend.* ***Jo*** *had that watch for several years. Later she always wanted bracelet watches, so I bought her the Deco Cuff Watch for Christmas one year. She only wore it on special occasions; being with* ***Jo*** *was always a special occasion for me.*

Cars – Our Sanctuary

Each weekday night after school, I worked at my Dad's used-car lot until 10 p.m. Then I would rush downtown; a 15 or 20 minute ride down Woodward, to pick up my beautiful **Jo** at the Broadway Capital Theater near Grand Circus Park. This was her part-time job after school. It was such a pleasure to see **Jo** heading for our car, night after night. I looked so forward to this routine, never tiring of it.

Mass transportation in Detroit, even then, had been a joke; anyone who had to rely on it could tell you that. With the roads fanning out from the half-wagon wheel pattern, it causes traffic tie-ups for trucks and buses, not to mention all of the cars. The street plan would have been vastly improved if it had been changed from a half-wagon wheel to a grid. Whenever **Jo** had to ride buses or streetcars, it would take her many long, hard, uncomfortable hours. If she had had to take public transportation every day, we would have had very little time with one another, but because I picked her up in our car, we were able to spend many contented hours together.

Jo tried to be home every night by midnight, so we still had an hour or two together before I had to get her home. We could have a snack, talk of the day's happenings, or plan for the next day's meetings which might include taking her to school, or to work, or to the library; we always asked what we could do for each other. Most of our lives **Jo** and I had energy to spare; together we could go day and night. We had become one person; our plans always meshed; that lasted for our entire life together.

In a few short weeks, I was to enter the Army Air Force. On the night this story takes place, I was picking **Jo** up at her part-time job as I had been doing for a long time now. We got something to eat and then parked in our favorite lover's lane to talk about our future. We were in love and no war was going to stop that. We snuggled close and talked about how we would write every day and think about each other every second of the day. At this time I'm still young and foolish, sure nothing could happen to me, telling **Jo** how I'd leap into the war and have it

*over in a couple of months; what did I know? I was just out of high school, **Jo** still in. We had so much to talk about that we wanted to spend all our time together. Whispering sweet things in each other's ears, holding each other, and being together was our only desire.*

*Mother had already met **Jo** and approved of our young love. She knew what time I was getting in every night and that it was getting later and later. She knew we were in love and we couldn't help it; time didn't matter to us. Dad, Baptist, had not met **Jo**, Catholic, yet and Mom knew that if they met under advantageous conditions Dad would love her as I did.*

*Meanwhile, **Jo** and I are holding on to each other, not wanting to let go. We were very comfortably snuggled together when we both slipped off to sleep. I'm not sure what woke us up, but waking up and realizing we had both been asleep for some time, caused sheer panic. "**Jo**, we've been asleep and it's very late," I said. "I'll get you home and then I've got to get home before Dad gets up or even the war will seem tame!" I was driving to work with Dad and our workday started very early in the morning.*

*I'm thinking fast on the ride home: "I'll have to fib if I'm caught in order to save **Jo's** reputation; it wasn't her fault, it was mine. How could I have fallen asleep? I'll say I had a flat tire; no, the car wouldn't start, I couldn't get to a phone." I pray I'm not caught, so I won't have to say anything. "Please, God," I pray, "get me out of this!" After kissing **Jo** and letting her out at her door, I flew home and parked the car, hoping it would cool down quick; we have to be off to work in less than an hour. I slipped in the front door as quietly as I could. There were no lights on. "Good." In the living room, I don't hear anything. "Great! Nobody up yet." I start up the steps to our bedrooms. I'm halfway up the stairs, when I see someone coming* *down. I hope it's Mom, but it's Dad. " Are you ready for work, Ken?" he says. Stunned I say, "yes, Sir," as I slip past him into the bathroom to wash my face before going into my bedroom to change clothes like it's just another day. Silently I say, "thank you, God." I'm sure Mother knew what time I got in, but she never said a word. She was covering up for us until the time when it wouldn't be necessary anymore. She respected our love and knew that in time Dad would see it all as she had.*

***Jo** and I agreed we would never do that again. Once was more than enough for both of us. I went to the store right away and purchased an alarm clock. We had only a few days to be together and we wanted to ensure peace at home before I went off to fight for peace in the world. I will always believe God wanted our love to grow. He protected us, so this true story could be told.*

*Once **Jo** and I were married, she never again rode on buses, streetcars, or even took a cab. Our cars, in our innocent youth, were our sanctuary and gave us great happiness. We parked in private, looked at the moon, the stars, and enjoyed the rain on the roof. We honored the meaning of sanctuary while making our great plans for the future. **Jo** being next to me made life worth-while. I always felt planning things with **Jo** was so joyous; she was always at the end of my imaginary rainbow. I know she is there still.*

Picking up Jo is what I
remember
beautiful June or slushy December
Her under the marquee
I was happy to see
It happened each night
with her smile so bright
We planned each day the night before
knowing a kiss was at her door
Receiving her love was such a delight
I knew of her love a moonlight flight
With success and devotion
we put our plans in motion
When you have a partner like Jo,
so wonderful only you know
She would never flaunt her success
giving me her love is what she did best.

Mother and Father

My astonishing Mother Leta and fantastic Father Alton saw that I got a good education and attended church every Sunday. Mother worked six days a week at the beauty salon she owned. Dad was very talented, worked two jobs most of his young life. He was a very good musician; people counted on him for entertainment until the radio came in. We always had friends or saw relatives Saturday nights or Sundays. Holidays meant family and guests getting together. I never heard Mother or Father swear or say anything out of the way. They could say the same about me. We had respect for one another.

The men played cards – no money involved. Hunting and fishing were talked about, the jobs they had, plans for the future. It was a complicated time, the depression. The women talked about sewing, cooking, canning. They were remarkable people striving for a better life.

I think a young man's life starts with his first steady girlfriend; I know mine did with **Jo**. The war was corrupt, but it cemented our love with over 2000 letters and getting together when we could. We were married shortly after I returned home from World War 11.

Jo and I met in 1941 and started dating in 1942. I left for air force pilot training on June 7, 1943; **Jo** started a diary that day. **Jo** and my Mother visited me at the University of Missouri in 1943. **Jo**, my Mother and Father visited me at a field in Illinois in July of 1944.

Jo moved in with my Mother and Dad. I received 47 letters at one mail call, most of them from **Jo**. In August of 1945 we knew the war would soon be over. All our letters were inexhaustible from that time on. Home in March, married to **Jo** on June 1st, 1946. That was the luckiest day of my life. I knew it then and I know it now. We spent our lives trying to please each other any way we could, wanting to better ourselves. I don't know of anyone we harmed in any way. If everyone was as harmonious as **Jo** was this would be almost Heaven on earth.

Mother and Jo

Excessively delicate, refined and beloved were Mother and **Jo** – so beautiful, so much alike. My Father and I had to be the luckiest husbands on earth. I didn't dream this up; I'll never understand why it had to end.

When **Jo** and Mother came to visit me when I was at the University of Missouri, they turned heads at that visit like I had never seen before. Mother at that time was compared to Joan Crawford, the movie star beauty. I had to keep the beautiful picture of **Jo** hidden because it drew too much attention and made me become jealous. I carried that picture and took care of it for years.

Mother and **Jo** never stayed in bed late. They were up and moving into life early every day. Both could always find something to do. They never went to bed early, always enjoying something until late into the night. I could not believe how they always would leave a room looking better for having been in it. If I moved a box or a bottle of perfume, **Jo** would notice and ask why. It was automatic for **Jo** and my Mother to know the place of everything.

Both took the time to look elegant, light with make-up, never painted on, selective and careful about apparel. Hair, hats and shoes had to be near perfect. From the bottom of their shoes to the top of their heads they cared how they looked, helping each other in all these preparations. They could suggest and compliment each other and it was a joy to witness how they could get along. They talked into the wee hours many, many nights discussing the past, the present and looking into the future. You know I always said it was very hard to outdo **Jo**, but my Mother was cut from the same cloth.

After Mother sold her beauty salon on 2nd avenue to one of the operators, she and Dad purchased a new home near the outskirts of

Detroit. **Jo** and I moved in with them as they insisted. It was a win-win situation for all of us. I had just returned from the war and wanted to spend time with Mother, Dad and **Jo**. In a new home you need a lot of help and **Jo** and I did all we could to make things as easy as possible for Mother and Dad.

In a few weeks we had made a great deal of progress, all of us enjoying every minute of it. **Jo** and I purchased a new bedroom set while Mother and Dad purchased new living and dining room furniture. Mother was so happy about the dining room because the house on Second Anenue didn't have one. It was what she had always wanted. Dad and I got a lawn started and put up a fence to keep our dog, Stormy, in our yard. The four of us, and our loyal dog, couldn't have been happier. We had good neighbors, too, who became life-long friends.

When we moved in with Mother
and Dad
what a joyous time all of us had
It was impossible to measure
that wonderful feeling of so much pleasure
Mother and Jo moving around
beauties in motion, what a happy sound
Dad commanding us to have more fun
anything we wanted was being done
For a short time we did Heaven see
they went ahead and are waiting for me.

Convertible

Dad started a used-car business in 1936. With the connections he had at Chrysler, he could get exceptional "supervisors" cars that had been treated very well and so seemed to most used-car buyers to be better than new. The used-car business at that time had a bad reputation, but Dad felt he would do great if he treated people right. Dad was a religious man, honest, and hard working. He wanted to treat people right and did. His plan was to get special cars, sell them to good people, and tell them that if they would take good care of them, he would buy them back later at a fair price. He could do this over and over, making a small profit each time, while still making a lot of good people happy. What could be better?

Mother was already working six days a week at her beauty shop; now Dad was working his job at Chrysler's to keep his connections and working six days at his car-lot. He was 39 years old when he was diagnosed as diabetic. It was difficult living with this medical condition,

but Dad always did the best he could and always tried to better himself and all those around him. He needed help at the used car lot, so he got me a special permit enabling me to drive for him while only 14 years old. I felt it was a great honor to be working with Dad, especially when he took me aside and told me how proud he was of me and the excellent job he knew I could do.

Dad employed Uncle Bert and Uncle Johnny, too, and that helped out the entire family. Uncle Bert was a fine man who married Daisy, my mother's sister. Uncle Johnny was my mother's only brother and he was always very good to her. Dad was doing great, with high sales and very happy customers. Everything was going according to his plan, but then World War 11 broke out; no more new cars, no more used cars, no more plan. The car lot closed, but now Dad was working overtime at Chrysler for the war effort.

Whenever Dodge Main was hiring, Dad would get jobs for the dependable people he knew. If you needed a job and he felt it would help you and the Corporation, he did whatever he could. Because of his sympathetic feeling for people and the loyalty he showed his company, all that dealt with Dad benefited. He was responsible for Chrysler's hiring over 200 good employees.

I was driving different cars off the lot, but was hoping for a car of my own that I could share with **Jo**. I had passed the test to become an Air Force Cadet and Dad was very proud of my accomplishment. He wasn't sure how long I would be home before leaving for the Army Air Force, but he wanted to get me a car of my own. He had only a few cars on his used-car lot, so he went to the newspaper.

One day Dad told me to be home at 4 p.m. "A young fellow is bringing a car by for your approval," he said. "He's going into the service right away and wants to sell his car." Our home shared a part of my Mother's beauty business, which fronted onto Second Avenue, a very busy one-way street. At this time of the day the traffic was so thick that a car couldn't stop on Second. I knew the young man would have to drive down Second Avenue and turn down a side street to park. I was watching all the cars; four lanes of them, hoping to see something **Jo** and I would like. The excitement grew. Dad hadn't told me anything about the color, make, or model, but I was sure he would pick a car for both **Jo** and I.

Just then a young man walked up to me and asked, "are you Ken Roberts?" I said, "yes," and he told me to follow him, that the car was parked on a side street. When I saw it, I couldn't believe this could be **Jo's** and mine. This was a very special car for my very beautiful girl and me. All at once I turned into a little boy, overwhelmed with joy. The young man said, " I hate to sell this, but I have been called up to serve." I told him about **Jo** and assured him that she and I would take good care of this wonderful car.

It was a Chrysler New Yorker Convertible, exceptional from top to bottom. It had a fluid drive transmission, also vacuum – matic; which meant you could shift gears without using the clutch. It had a great radio and heater and a special plate to keep water from stalling you out. It had winter or summer seat covers, wrap around dashboard and musical horns. It, also, had Puncture-proof inner-tubes for the full white sidewalls and over-size tires.

This guy had good taste, plus the car had only a few miles on it, better than new. With **Jo** driving, all eyes would be on her. "Wait till **Jo** has a look at this marvelous car of ours," I thought. The young man, after running his hands along the side of his car, handed the keys to me and said that if I took him home, the car was mine. I drove him home to Grosse Pointe and as I drove home in my new car I was the happiest boy on this planet. Dad had made all the arrangements, so I didn't have to do anything or wait even a minute. Mother was delighted that Dad had gone out of his way to make me so happy. By now you understand what a marvelous family I had; add **Jo** and you're sure to know why I want to be with them this second.

The night I picked **Jo** up from work in the Chrysler New Yorker convertible that Dad and Mom had arranged to buy for me, I told her it was ours. Love works in strange and glorious ways when you respect and desire each other above all things. **Jo's** name was a part of me. We would talk about everything, enjoying learning all about each other's family, church, school, work, and friends. The time we spent together would just fly by, then a goodnight kiss and a promise to see each other the next day.

Life was so wonderful with my **Jo** and she told me she felt the same way. I couldn't understand why **Jo** picked me over so many guys, but I felt fortunate that she had. "I'm not half good enough for her," I'd think, "I just won't tell her what I think about myself; I'll just do the best I can every day we're together and try to be worthy of her love." We were always so happy in one another's arms. Our romance lasted over 55 years.

When I eventually went into the service Dad took great care of the convertible, letting **Jo** have it any time he could. They could only operate one car because of gas rationing. **Jo** was now working at the same plant as Dad, so they could both ride to work in it. **Jo** used the car to drive Mother any place she wanted to go. Almost everyone was working seven days a week trying to supply the troops and win the war as quickly as possible. Dad and **Jo** had a new top put on our car and they took turns washing it. They each wrote letters to me all about the good care they were taking of our car, so that when I returned we would still have the convertible to drive around in that we enjoyed so much.

Although we were all comfortable living together in our big house on Second, Dad and Mother knew that **Jo** and I needed our own things to feel independent. When the war ended, Dad ordered a new car for him and Mom, so **Jo** and I could have the convertible back. This six-year old car had served us well, but it needed a lot of work. Because the automobile plants hadn't started to remanufacture convertibles yet, Dad helped us get a new Plymouth Club Coupe.

When they did come out with convertibles, a good friend of ours went to the auto dealership at the same time so we could order two and get a better deal. We both had those cars for some time enjoying them very much. We have some of the pictures of us in the two cars that we cherish to this day. With **Jo's** guidance we had almost anything we really wanted. When **Jo** first saw the car she was overwhelmed with happiness. In all our lives, love grew stronger with everything we got involved with.

Dad and Mother's Gift

Dad's love of cars extended to us
spending so much, without a fuss
Jo and I were overwhelmed
with the person at the helm
Mother told us of her great joy
Dad and her gift to that girl and boy
The gift brought this family together
"top-up" to protect you from the weather
To enjoy our sanctuary, we needed a car
"top-down" to enjoy the moon and stars
Seeing thousand's of stars in heaven above
this present came with Mother and Dad's love.

What If?

I was with some friends having a sandwich and a malt near my church when a friend asked if he could borrow our convertible. Wally said he wanted to make an impression on his girlfriend. "You can have the keys to my new car," he said, "until I get back, just in case you need a car." I figured he had insurance and money and he was my friend. We went to the same church on the next block and **Jo** was not involved, so I tossed him the keys. "What could possibly go wrong?" I thought. He was gone for only a few minutes, but still I was so glad when he brought our car back. "I won't do that again," I thought, "I'm so pleased that's over." It felt wrong to have someone else driving our car.

Don, the friend who stayed with me while Wally was out driving my car, asked me for a ride home and I said, "sure, hop in." On the way to his house, I slowed down to look in the window of a restaurant we sometimes found our buddies frequenting. Suddenly a guy standing on the sidewalk took a swing at Don. We didn't even know the guy! As soon as I saw this, I sped away, wondering all the while what was going on. The guy jumped into a car with a bunch of his friends, all shouting things we couldn't understand. The chase was on, but over what? I wasn't able to lose them on the side streets, so I cut over to Woodward, a main street, and mixed in with heavy traffic. I finally lost them.

Don had heard the guy in the other car hollering something which made him think that Wally was somehow involved in all this. I waited in Don's living room while he called Wally on the phone. Sure enough, Wally confessed that he had tried to pick up a girl he didn't know; she must have told someone and given them a description of my Chrysler convertible. We both gave Wally a piece of our mind because we didn't do things like that. As he hung up the phone, Don told me he thought he recognized one of the guys chasing us, that he'd been in a classroom *with him. A couple of days later, he went to the restaurant and talked to the young man, telling him about my owning the convertible and having nothing to do with what happened. They came to an agreement and Don told me the hunt was off! Was I ever glad!*

I told ***Jo*** *what had happened and we agreed that no one was to ever borrow our car again. We played what if? What if ... those guys had caught us, what if ... they had smashed our car? what if ... the police had gotten involved? what if ... my Dad found out? what if ... I had gone to jail? what if ... the Army Air Force had found out? All these what if's frightened me so much, I told* ***Jo*** *I would never do anything like that again. Wally was wrong to do what he did, but I shouldn't have loaned him our car in the first place. When you're a responsible person, think of all the possible what if's? On* ***Jo's*** *desk at work she had three signs, "****Jo Roberts****," "Think," and "Heaven will protect the working girl." Heaven is protecting my* ***Jo****, right now, as always.*

Night after Night

It's 10 p.m. – time to pick up **Jo**. I start our dark blue New Yorker Convertible at my Dad's lot on Livernois and drive South on Woodward, careful not to break the speed limit. The police are always watching for young drivers in flashy convertibles; I have Dad to answer to and I don't want him angry with me. As I drive, I think about **Jo**. The back window is down, because it's a hot night. I have already tuned the radio to our favorite music station. We will listen to Glen Miller, I hope, as he is **Jo's** current favorite; maybe some Sinatra, too.

The car is so clean it gleams; I worked on it most of the night, wanting **Jo** to be impressed, pleased with my efforts. The glass is so clean you're not even sure it's there. When I drive under the marquee at the theater where **Jo** works, the light is so bright the car sparkles, almost half as much as **Jo**. I am so proud of my pretty young girlfriend and the class she adds to the overall picture as she walks under the marquee towards me, smiling and waving.

Drive-ins are the thing for a quick snack or a malt-to-go for a little later in the evening. Everyone looks at us – that beautiful girl and that shiny new convertible car. You have no idea how good **Jo** makes me feel. This has been a great day, and now an even better night, having my **Jo** beside me.

We arrive at Belle Isle and get a good parking place; some of the regulars are already there. I turn off the motor and "String of Pearls" is playing on the radio. I am so happy being with my **Jo**. We've talked on the ride over, how we missed each other and how much we love each *other. We embrace for about an hour, peaceful and quite with one another; it is so nice holding* ***Jo*** *in my arms, night after night. Could things be better?*

The moon is glistening on the water, the stars are sparkling so bright, and the music is playing so soft; surely God has blessed us tonight. Sinatra is singing " I've got a crush on you," and" I've got the world on a string." Now "Blue Champagne" and "Tuxedo Junction" by Glen Miller is playing. In my mind's eye, I can see Miller's band resplendedly dressed in their long white jackets. If they ever come to town, I resolve to see them with ***Jo*** *at my side.*

The music is so soft, I'm sure God in his heaven loves this and I just know in my heart that he wants ***Jo*** *and I together forever. The two or three hours we spend together each night is blessed. Life is good and worth living. We plan ahead for tomorrow and the coming week. When all the details are talked over, it's time to take* ***Jo*** *home. We share a tender goodnight kiss at her door, then a soft, "I love you, see you tomorrow!" Driving home I am the happiest man on earth, night after starry night.*

Youth is such joy
for the right Girl and Boy
We don't mind the weather
in our desire to be together
Nothing can stop our love
that comes from above
Each night of bliss
sealed with Jo's kiss
Back tomorrow to start again
Never any sorrow with Jo and Ken
Love till tomorrow she has given her guarantee
so hard to understand why she saves it for me
Jo was the purpose he gave me to live
so I don't question God when he gives
my joy with Jo will never end
When God brings us together again.

Harry "The Indian" Altman

My Dad was a fine religious man, so you wouldn't think he'd ever know a gangster well enough to say hello to, but you'd be wrong. He was the secretary of the Chrysler Gun Club and that is where he met Harry "the Indian" Altman, a known member of "the Purple Gang," a local Detroit gang of thugs.

At age 17, I had just graduated from High School and had enrolled in the Chrysler job training school. I had plans to go into the Army Air Force pilot training program as soon as I could. I was scheduled to take the entrance exam, but couldn't enlist until I reached the age of 18. I rode to work each day with Dad, because his status as supervisor gave him a private parking space. He worked longer hours than I did, so he arranged for me to stay in a private room inside a neighborhood bar across the street until he could drive us both home. The room was small and furnished with only a table and four chairs. I could do school work or relax; it was much better than sitting outside in a cold car.

I was in the room alone one day, when Harry "the Indian" Altman walked in. He wasn't tall, but he was big and very solidly built, like a healthy young bull. You knew right away that you did not want to tangle with this man. He wasn't bad looking except for the deep scar across his cheek. "Who are you?" he asked. "Ken Roberts," I answered. "So you're Alton's son," he said, " I like your Dad." Just then Dad walked in and I watched in amazement as they exchanged greetings like any two old friends.

On the ride home Dad said to me, "Harry's a good friend to have, but don't ever joke with him." "He doesn't like jokes?" I asked. "If you were to point at someone," Dad explained, " and you said you don't like that person," Harry, being your friend, might make the guy disappear.

Be very careful what you say to that man. I'll tell you about Harry," he continued, "he is the #1 Purple Gangster. His name is in the papers all the time. He is involved with very bad people. He's a gun for hire and likes to hurt people." "Why isn't he in the service then?" I asked innocently. Dad laughed and said, "you can't enter the service if you have a Police record, son. Please, Ken; don't ask him about the service. He wants to fight, but they won't let him." I didn't ask any more questions, as Dad seemed eager to change the subject.

I ended up spending a lot of time with Harry that winter. His job was to carry money from the stores, bars, banks, and payroll, to cash checks for the factory workers. Almost everyone was working overtime and that meant a lot of money was moving around. Harry was "paid protection." He would help cash checks on payday and told me to always come to his window. They had three windows where long lines would form. They called out the money they gave you as they cashed your check. Since almost everyone got about the same amount of money, nobody really cared if the others knew how much you made. When I had a check for $65.50 Harry would call out very loudly 100 dollars for each 10 dollars I had. "One hundred, two hundred, three hundred, four hundred, five hundred, six hundred and fifty dollars," he'd holler and most of the men in the line would hear it. As I walked back through the room, I could hear them saying incredulously, " that young kid makes $650.00? Wonder what he does?" I would duck into the private room before anyone could ask me directly. Harry told me that as a precaution, he would walk Dad and me out to the car on payday. He'd quickly added, "but don't tell your dad why, it's a little secret just between you and me, pal." I quickly agreed with anything Harry suggested.

I told Harry about **Jo** and showed him her picture. I asked him how I could take care of myself against a bully or somebody big like him. He said, "kid, first, run as fast as you can. If you know the guy's *name, get a letter to him and tell him to watch the papers, tell him your best friend is Harry "the Indian" Altman. Tell him that if something happens to me, or my beautiful girlfriend," he went on, "a letter will be sent to my best friend, Harry, and you will soon meet him and you'll wish you hadn't for the rest of your life!" It's funny how much safer I felt after that, just knowing Harry called me his best friend.*

A couple of years later, I was in the service. On a visit home on a ten-day furlough before going over-seas, Dad took me back to Chrysler's to meet with some of his co-workers. Afterward, I stopped by the Flying Duck Bar and asked about Harry; I was told he was in jail for not taking a defense job. Every able-bodied man was expected to work in the war effort or he went to jail. Since he couldn't get in the Army and wouldn't take the defense job when it was offered, Harry went to jail. Harry had been a good friend to Dad and me. I hope God will consider how well Harry treated us. I told **Jo** *about Harry, that summer and what we had talked about so many years ago.* **Jo** *said, "it's so sad that people can't be friends with everyone." She understood perfectly the friendship that had formed between a young man just out of high school and this Purple Gangster.* **Jo** *was happy I didn't get hurt, but had made a friend.*

Pilot Training

It was a terrible war and would go on for some time yet, because we were losing it to Germany and Japan. They were cheering and we were tearing. Having passed the test for pilot training and having had the operation to improve my breathing, I was leaving for duty in the U.S. Army Air Force. It was so sad to be leaving **Jo** and my loving parents. On the way to the train station, I drove by **Jo's** house, silently saying, "I love you, **Jo**." Dad knew this was not the way to the train station, but didn't say anything. He knew **Jo** lived in the area and that I was thinking of her. He had not yet truly accepted **Jo** and wasn't sure how things would turn out. At the train station, I turned to shake hands with Dad. He told me to be a good pilot and to honor the Roberts name. He said he was very proud of me, would write and work all he could to end this horrible war, bringing me safely back home again. I could see he was hurting, then he turned to drive home alone.

Basic army training for me was in Wichita Falls, Texas. I had never seen so many men bunked down in airplane hangers and prefabricated houses. There were formations for everything, including getting in line for shots; you saw thousands and thousands of soldiers, but only a few cadets. Everywhere you looked, men marching, standing in lines for everything. Everyone acted like a group of cattle, no one knowing what to do. It was always,"hurry up and wait," never knowing anything for sure; up early rushing around, chow, exercise on the run, always double-time.

We had a very fine Sergeant, who was exceptional to us. He made us perform better than the rest, never embarrassing our squadron in front of other recruits. We witnessed some of the rougher Sergeants and came to appreciate ours even more. Completing basic training, we were shipped to the University of Missouri for Aeronautical Engineering. From there we were sent to San Antonio, our classification center. I classified as a pilot, bombardier and navigator; since I was allowed to choose what I wanted, I happily selected pilot.

As cadets we were up early for breakfast, then physical training (pt), and classes in pre-flight school, aircraft recognition, maps and charts, training films, Morse code, radio communication, and many other subjects. We marched in formation to everything, and were never allowed to wander around. Orders were posted on a board continuously, our duty assignments. Nothing was done incidentally; they wanted it all planned. Every minute of the day and night was accounted for from reveille to lights-out. All decisions about what we cadets did were at the discretion of our Officers. Cultivating discipline was what it was all about. I could write a letter home if we were waiting for something or on a break. Sunday was Church service and being confined to your area. This rule was only broken with permission which was not easy to obtain, though it was easier for cadets who had a parent in town. On Sundays we would go to the day room and get in line for a phone to call home or we would spend the afternoon writing letters home, playing cards or visiting with our buddies.

We took a train from San Antonio to a flying school near Bonham, Texas, which had been a private training school for civilians before the war. It was training, schooling, and flying under strict army command with the same officers we had at the base near Kelly Field. A very fine elderly gentleman and his wife owned the flying school and the Army Air Force leased this facility from him for the duration of the war. At an assembly, he informed us that he had the army agree to some changes, all in favor of the cadets who would

fly from his fields. We would be treated special – no G.I. haircuts, not long hair, mind you, but cut to look neat, the cafeteria would be staffed with young women and chef's from the town of Bonham, and if we felt something was unjust, we could go see him day or night. Each night this lovely couple invited four different cadets to have dinner with them. All of us, at some time or other, would set at their dining room table. They were upper class in all ways.

I had set my goal to become a P-39 Airacobra pilot. This was an airplane with a cannon in a single propeller. The cockpit was small because the propeller shaft came from the in-line engine that was behind the pilot. This gave smaller pilots like me one up on the big guys. The Airacobra had one bad fault, however; it was prone to flat spins because of the placement of the engine and it would take some special training to be able to fly one. I'm 18, gung ho; I had no fear, which is equal to no common sense. I know that now, but didn't then. I thought I would be in a squadron that was invincible. "We'll win the war in ninety days, and come home hero's, let's do it," I thought.

Each instructor at Bonham was assigned four cadets. The instruction officer assigned to my group was Lt. O'Mally. He wore glasses because his vision wasn't 20-20, so he couldn't qualify for Air Force Cadet. Lt. O'Mally wanted us to be the best and gave us all his attention. He was the one who had to prepare us to solo, an awesome job. I felt he treated us like younger brothers. He was hard on us, but tempered his lessons with kindness. He taught us maneuvers that he felt would save our lives in combat. It's not possible to explain how we looked up to him.

Thinking back on the planes that we were learning to fly I realize that these Fairchild primary trainers had no push buttons and very few instruments. That would come much later. They were great planes for their day; something like the Model T. was for the early auto industry. You had to manually and manfully fly these under-powered machines and physical coordination was everything. The wrong move and they would stall out. If you were near the ground, you would crash. Your instructors would take you up a few thousand feet to practice, so every student pilot had a safety net. Landings and takeoff's were the real problems, as there was no safety net then.

I had something wonderful even then that I didn't realize – **Jo** was my co-pilot, she was always with me. Communicating with **Jo** daily by writing her and always wanting to do my best so I could tell her about my success helped me to become a success. If you had a pin-up, sweetheart or loved one, you had a Co-pilot; mine was named Jo.

While I was stationed in Bonham, some West Point cadets moved in to the barracks connected to mine. These were four-year trained cadets from the finest facility in the world. We understood that they had been given this rare opportunity by the Army Air Force to go up in several types of planes, but none of them would become pilots or be given pilot training. We never found out exactly why they were there, but we knew they hadn't been off the West Point campus in over four years. They ate in the same cafeteria as us and seemed to enjoy talking to us about anything we asked. They stayed to themselves mostly, because they were superior to us; we all knew this, too, and secretly wished we could be as good as them. My squadron shared the same wash rooms with them. I was so glad **Jo** and my mother weren't able to see the comparison.

Photos of the cadets that had graduated before us hung on the wall of the cafeteria. Most of us looked at the photographs. I was so naive at that time that when I saw gold stars by their photos I assumed it meant they were "outstanding." Moving slowly along in the line to eat, we spent much time looking at these fine flyers and it brought the war very close to home when we realized that the stars meant these cadets were dead or missing. Seeing so many gold stars and knowing those cadets had stood in a line like this, at this very school, made us grow up fast. Reality set in very quickly after that. None of us wanted a gold star.

During the course of the war, it seemed like Germany, Japan and Italy were taking over the world. The average person had no idea what, or if, an atomic bomb could ever be invented; they didn't even know the word atomic. Can you believe that? Atomic means smallest, infinitesimal, tiniest, and even microscopic. What could that have to do with ending a World War? Two years later, with the war in Europe still raging, President Harry Truman said yes to the atomic bomb. He saved my life with that answer. I'm sorry that so many innocent people were killed, but all wars are horrible. Remember the U.S. of A. didn't start this war. God doesn't want the monsters of this world to rule. Love and caring about each other is what people should be thinking about. My Angel **Jo** was for everything good. That's why I miss her so much, I can't wait to be with her. I want my gold star.

Pilot Training

I get my gold star and join my Jo
the only place I want to go
Floating in clouds, so soft and clean
holding hands in our glider of dreams
Our love is so strong it will last forever
yet we don't weight as much as a feather
We found our glorious life
Jo is back to being my wife.

Jo was my Pinup

As a Cadet in the Army Air Force, I had to live up to very high standards. We had Officers and Instructors who monitored our every action. When we marched to Church on Sunday stepping out of line was not tolerated. We had to walk a straight and narrow path in everything we did. We had pride in our squadron, our parents and the pinup back home.

Throughout the years I was in the service I carried **Jo's** picture in my barracks bag, which traveled with me through most of the United States, the Pacific Islands, and Korea. I protected my pinup with my life and I know **Jo** protected me through the power of love. The picture I carried was a portrait; **Jo** had a beautiful body, but she would not pose for that kind of picture. She was shy and never felt she was beautiful, but all the cadets who saw her photo disagreed.

When I first set her picture out near my bunk, it attracted way too much attention from the rest of the guys. From that time on, I saved it for myself and a select few friends. I was too envious at that time of my

life to share ***Jo****. I wore that picture out and didn't have a copy; fortunately, I married the real thing and lived happily ever after. If we had been married at the time and I knew her better, I might have felt differently. In fact, after we were married a few years, I changed my position completely. I wanted everybody in the world to know my* ***Jo****.*

It was people like Mother, Dad and ***Jo*** *who won World War 11. Could we have won it without them? I don't think so. I needed my wonderful parents and my pinup,* ***Jo****. I can never thank them enough, but I will still try. In my next life, I will have a lot to say to them, all of it with love. When you have great parents and a wonderful pinup girl, no tyrant will ever win against you. The young people of today have no idea what it was like then, the evil power in the world that was overcome by courageous, loving people. Those pinup girls worked hard in the war effort inspiring the young lovers to never give up. It was a time I didn't like, but one I'll never forget mainly because of my pinup girl.*

Pinup

Jo could not help knowing she had beautiful hair
always giving it phenomenal care
Sparkling blue eyes; very smooth skin
perfect structure from forehead to chin
If you praised her, she would blush
I can hear her saying: "Aw, Ken, you hush"
Look at her picture and notice the smile
something Cadets were sure to admire
She was a pinup for quite a few
then my jealousy removed Jo's photo from view

Heroic Effort

I feel that Mother, Dad and **Jo**, through their heroic effort, were responsible for my surviving World War 11. They are the unsung heros. The time and devotion to the war effort that they gave to this country saved a lot of lives.

As a boy, I had built a lot of model airplanes and hoped to pilot a real one someday. Since I only weighed 125 lbs. at graduation, my dad agreed with me that I would have a much better chance to do more for the country as a pilot. I took the tests, but I had a minor medical problem that kept me from passing the breathing test. My parents paid for the operation I needed to enlarge my nasal passages enabling me to pass the test when I took it again.

Japan had done such a horrible thing – killing innocent people not far from the United States in a sneak attack on Pearl Harbor. None of us wanted the war, but when Uncle Sam says, "I need you," you honor your country. I honored my family, **Jo** and my country with the 34 months I served being the best soldier I could be. I wanted to stop them before they bombed my family or **Jo**. We had friends that were killed in the war and I like to think our combined efforts saved other's from sacrificing their lives.

Jo and I hugged and kissed the night before I left, crying and promising to do our very best. She told me she would pray for me, that everything would be all right; she never told me anything that wasn't true. My mother wasn't a physically strong person except when she hugged and kissed me good-bye; I was her only child and she hated to see me go, knowing all the while that I had to. Dad gave me a hug, a handshake, and told me to be a good pilot.

They gave me all the support they could, writing and visiting me whenever possible. Communication from home was so important to the men in the field. Could I have had better parents? NO. Could I had a better girlfriend? NO. The Officers of my squadron planned my life in the Army Airforce for me. I could only do what I was told, but there was good food for pilots, as well as schooling, testing, flying all planned for us. When they called, "lights out," I got all the sleep I required.

Dad worked with Chrysler Corporation in the war effort right from the start to end the war as soon as possible. Mother, Dad, and **Jo** purchased all the war bonds they could; doing everything our government said was necessary to end the terrible war. They worked day and night. I read that in **Jo's** diary; none of them told me how hard they worked. I never knew of **Jo's** diary until recently. When I read that **Jo** waited in the snow and rain for a bus transfer for over 45 minutes, I cried. I never wanted **Jo** to suffer any hardship.

To bed near midnight, up at 5:30 a.m. **Jo**, Mother and Dad making breakfast on the run. **Jo** to school, my parents to work rain or shine; they were always working for the war effort. Rationing was standard practice and there was nothing plentiful, but bad news. Hitler's Germany and Tojo's Japan were on the move killing young men and women at a horrible rate. The bad news was tearing at my parents and **Jo** everyday.

Lines formed everywhere, as there were shortages of food, clothing, and gasoline. Almost everything was needed for the war effort. Transportation was very poor and in short supply. The war had turned the world upside down for us in this picturesque country. The wonderful joy here on earth stopped, pain and suffering was growing at a terrifying rate and people were being hurt day and night. The pain would last forever for some remarkable peace loving people whose loved ones had been badly hurt or killed on the battlefields. Lives were broken and torn apart; Germany and Japan were cheering while the rest of the world screamed in pain. The young people of the future will never know the heroic effort that was needed to get Hitler and Tojo out for the count, unless we tell them about people like Mother, Dad and **Jo**, and families like them. Everyone hurting so much, but saving a world from the sick monsters. In Heaven we will never be apart again or hurt anyone again. We will have what Mother, Dad, **Jo** and I wanted from the start, love. I won't have to **remember my Jo**; I'll be with her.

Being a good soldier you do as you're
told
following orders; that's the code
If you step out of line, that's an infraction
this will prepare you for military action
Mother, Dad, and Jo
because of the war, always on the go
Their heroic effort night and day
is why we still have a U.S. of A.
They'll do what it takes to win any war
keeping the enemy away from our shore
Always sad that they had to hurt
but you can be sure they will never desert
When your push comes to shove
they'll still end it with love
That's all they wanted from the start
God didn't want you to break their heart.

Her Letters started

↓

Dearest Kenney:

Hi, Sweetheart.

Her Letter ended

↓

My letters started

Darling Jo,

My letters ended

I love, I miss you, I need you,

Always yours if you want me.

Love Kenney

GOOD NIGHT BEAUTIFUL

I get so excited about you coming home. I can just imagine how nice it will be. Hubba-Hubba- You for me forever.

It's getting late and I still have to put my hair up- so for tonite and until I see you again I'm →

Always yours,

Love Jo

Mrs. K. Roberts

Goodnite Sweetheart.

Kenney - Jo Sandy Trisha Delight

2-0309

Letters from Jo

Jo's handwriting was smooth, like her voice. When I read her letters the way they are written, it's as if she is talking to me. It's a skill I wish I had. She said I had it, but I didn't feel I had it. Maybe it's connected with the love we had for each other.

Most of the letters I'm reading now are from World War 11. I was moving around a lot and some of the letters would get to me out of date. When I did read her letters it was as if she was reading them to me. I could hear her voice and the expressions she used wasn't her writing, but her speaking. It's a joy to read her letters now because her voice is still in the words. The little quips in her love letters to me are so special at this time and I remember how wonderful each letter she wrote was to me then.

Her rushing to get letters off each day, writing in her diary, doing homework for school, off to a part-time job, keeping a scrap book, riding street cars, buses, near 20 miles a day, seeing her friends, her family, and my parents. **Jo** didn't have much time for sleep; it's in her diary that I hadn't known she kept.

When **Jo** wrote to me I didn't have to read between the lines, because her descriptions were so accurate. Mail call was my high each day; I was sure to get a letter or one was on the way, or maybe even two or three. I knew it was not **Jo's** fault if I didn't get a letter. We would talk on the phone occasionally, but it wasn't something you could count on. Lines for the phone sometimes would be a three and four hour wait. Millions in the service and not enough phone lines. Only certain days you could phone – always army business.

Writing was so important and if you had time you could read them over and over again. We saved most of our two thousand plus letters *and gifts. **Jo** and I talked about reviewing them one day when we got old and had the time. We never got old or had the time.*

*To me **Jo's** letters were blessed, as were the words she spoke to me. **Jo** had such a special way of saying things. To **Jo**, good things were "yum, yum" and "huba, huba" meant she was happy. When I read, "Isn't my dress yummy, Ken?" or "hubba, hubba, our new car is ready," I cry with joy because I can hear her voice in those words. Her joy and her excitement always expressed her love. I was always so happy being near her and hearing her say, "Aw, Ken," with a little laugh.*

She started each letter to me:
"Dearest Kenney,
Hi, Sweetheart"

*I started each letter to **Jo**:*
*"Darling, **Jo**"*

Her endings were always different, but always wonderfully filled with so much love and imagination.

Most of the time mine said,
"I love you, miss you, need you.
Always Yours, if you want me,
Love, Kenney."

I only wish they had a post office in Heaven.

Honeymoon

Jo was so gorgeous as my bride when we got married on Saturday, June 1 st, 1946, at Our Lady of Rosary Church,

5860 Woodward Avenue, Detroit, Michigan. It was our dream of 5 years culminating with this wonderful event. I know God saw **Jo** that day, because she stood out like a jewel in his flock; he couldn't possibly have missed her.

My parents' deep and abiding love for **Jo** and I had been the reason why they searched out a wonderful spot for our honeymoon called Potawatomi Inn in Angola, Indiana. It was a beautiful hotel in Northern Indiana set on 1,040 acres of Pakagon State Park; the Inn was a private facility separate from the State Park, a very exclusive place in 1946. We made the trip there the two happiest people on Earth.

Potawatomi Inn stood high above Lake James, surrounded by orchards filled with wild birds, elk, deer, and buffalo, picnic grounds, tennis courts, an archery range, and golf courses. There was swimming, canoeing, and fishing, too. There was no end to what you could do with the assistance of the staff at the Inn. They planned things for you, but would also leave you alone if you so desired. Since it was June, we couldn't use the toboggan run, but we did walk the heavenly nature trail beside it. We planned to return one day just to reminisce, to see if some of our love was still there; sadly, that never happened.

I don't understand why the happy times have to rush by so fast. I can't really remember how many days we were there, but I do remember the beauty. The tall green trees, the deep-blue water, the endless expanse of grass and the sky an immaculate vault of heaven. How ***Jo's*** *blue eyes sparkled, the joy she radiated in everything she did. Everything we saw and felt was exceptional. Our honeymoon was magnificent, as glorious as the love we felt for one another.*

The joy I want in Heaven would be to relive those great times with my ***Jo*** *in very slow motion. The life I had with* ***Jo*** *was so wonderful, but I know now that it just rushed by. Whenever I was waiting to see* ***Jo****, I was like a little boy waiting for Christmas. That's how I feel now – that time isn't passing fast enough to suit me.*

A Honeymoon is a very special time
for a very good reason everything rhymes
Colors are brighter, the future so clear
a new start in life that you travel each year
If you treat each other as you vowed you would
looking at cloudy days, you'll find some good
Savor each moment of your Honeymoon
celebrate your Anniversary each and every June
Don't ever put away
the memory of that day
If you keep it in your mind
everything will be fine
Jo was my lifeline to happiness
this to her I had to confess
She always knew that I loved her so
giving love back in the name of Jo
Heaven processes how you begin
if you need to find us, just look for Jo and Ken.

Picture of Jo

Spark

Jo inspired me. In her loving way, she was a force for anything good. When **Jo** talked to me, I sparked. She set off things in my mind that I wanted to do because of her. I always had an open mind when **Jo** was involved. I can't say why, except I loved her so much. I always rushed to do the things I had to do in order to get the time for **Jo**'s desires.

Sleeping next to **Jo** was always my pleasure. I don't think I ever woke up sad. I was slow to wake, but with **Jo** around, it was always a good start. Her voice, her presence, the knowledge that we were okay made life wonderful. **Jo** loved life so much that even our chores seemed not at all bad because we were together. The "aw, Ken" with a little laugh was always in the future.

I talk a lot; **Jo** was the quiet type, never interrupting. When **Jo** did talk, it meant a lot to me. I always wanted to know her opinion or her desires. When **Jo** said, "Let's build a new house," I sparked and we started. When she later said, "a recreation room," I sparked and we started again. Then "a spa room" and we were off and running again. **Jo** would do more than her share and the thing would get completed.

We always found time for each other every day of our lives. **Jo** was retired for 15 years and I for 10. Those were the wonderful years for **Jo** to spark my mind. I wish it had lasted for an eternity. I have to say the spark has gone out of my life now. Soon, when **Jo** and I are together again, it will light up the heavens. I hope that when you look at the night sky you will **remember my Jo**.

Jo and Improvement

*What color did **Jo** like? It had to be white. We had 10 new white cars. "I'll keep them clean, Ken," she'd tell me, and she always did. Oh, she liked to see the contrast of colors, but she also wanted places that would normally be dark to look clean, white and bright.*

*I have said before and will say again now **Jo** always wanted things to improve. One time, in her efforts to keep things clean, she even said she would like to own a car wash. I knew that if she did, she would be successful, but she would work much too hard and not at paper work either! I'm thankful she didn't get her hands on a microscope too often here on earth. I would sometimes jokingly tell her that when she got to Heaven, everything would just keep getting cleaner. I'm sure that if that's true, **Jo** is a very happy lady right about now. She would pitch in and do any and every job that needed to be done; simply making the improvement without drawing any attention to it.*

*We didn't compliment each other in front of other people, nor did we criticize. We so seldom had anything to criticize, because we talked things over before we did anything significant. We always felt that some input from the other was a good way of saying, "I love you and want your opinion on this." You can tell from my love for **Jo** that I would do any deed she asked, yet she did not need my permission; likewise, if **Jo** stopped me from doing what I was pursuing, it was because she could see a better way. Later in life, I would admit that she had been right and I had been wrong. I didn't when I was younger; that had to be learned from my remarkable **Jo**. I became a better person because of my **Jo**. Much of her good has rubbed off on me.*

Wedding in Philadelphia

I met Joe Panichelli in the South Pacific during World War 11. When the war was over, we took some classes together. He was a very fine person-polite, friendly, and religious – and we became the best of friends. We had a lot of things in common. He was an only child like me, his parents wanted him to attend college, and he desired to make this world a better place. We talked about what life would be like when we got home and hoped we could still be friends back in the States. I knew he had a nice family from the love he showed for them. His father owned a barbershop. Joe's hard-working parents were good people, desiring life to be better for their son.

Jo and I were writing everyday, talking about getting married in all our letters, when one day she wrote back, "pick a best man." Joe was Catholic like my **Jo**, so I knew he would be perfect if we were both sent home at the same time. I asked him and he said after seeing **Jo's** picture and what I had told him about her, he would gladly circle the globe for a chance to see her. Joe went home to Philadelphia, but he came to Detroit to be my best man like he said he would. We had a very small wedding, so Joe rushed into town for that weekend, then quickly returned to Philadelphia to attend law school again on Monday.

About three years later, **Jo** and I received an invitation to attend the Panichelli wedding. Joe had finished his college education and was taking a bride. **Jo** and I were both working, but decided we could make the trip on the weekend. We had just purchased a new convertible, so making a trip to see a friend get married would be grand. How proud I would be for everyone to meet my marvelous **Jo**. When you loved someone like I loved **Jo**, you wanted others to share the joy of her presence. We got off early Friday and drove to Philadelphia in a rush.

Driving into an older section of Philadelphia, I stopped at a corner gas station to ask directions. The attendant asked if I knew the location of the old prison, that that was near where Joe lived. Back in the car, I didn't dare tell **Jo** what we were looking for. When she saw the high walls, the searchlights, and guard towers, I had to tell her. Looking at each other, we saw that we were frightened at being out of our element. I found the street and cautiously proceeded to look for the address. All we could see everywhere we looked were tenement houses, blocks of them; I had never seen anything like this before, except in movies. Every street corner had large groups of young men milling around, which didn't look inviting. Then I saw a barber pole and the name "Panichelli" written on the storefront window. The address was correct, but there was no place to park, so I drove off. We drove a few miles further and found a new motel where we gladly checked in. I called the Panichelli home and got Joe. He said he was happy to hear we had arrived, then proceeded to give me directions to the church for the next morning. It was a beautiful day for a wedding. The wedding was huge and held in a beautiful old Church that had stood the test of time very well.

We got special treatment being from out-of-town. We were to go with the bridal procession. We formed a long line of cars as we left the church, and drove to a fancy hall where some local dignitaries were waiting. We had a huge breakfast, drank several toasts, and listened to speeches, all praising the Panichelli family. Joe's father was obviously deeply involved in local politics. His parents were very young, nice-looking, and intensely friendly. We drove to five different homes with the caravan, eating special food at each one that had been especially prepared for us. The tenements that had looked so bad in the dark of night were beautiful inside consisting of several big rooms with high ceilings. I'm sure they had been done over. Never judge a book by its cover; I never did again after seeing the beauty inside those places. The bridal group went to have their pictures taken, while we went to another house to eat. You had to eat or you would offend them and the family at each home wanted you to eat even more. Italian people love to eat; I found that out that day and night.

We had an enormous spaghetti lunch, with many side dishes and special meat dishes. It's been said: "If you ever found a girl who looked good eating spaghetti, marry that lady." **Jo** always looked good eating spaghetti and I was the luckiest man on earth to have married her.

Several people asked us if we had seen the bedroom? Each group we came to asked the same question – "Have you seen the bedroom?" I had never heard an expression like that and was stunned by its obvious implications. Finally, we were told what "seeing the bedroom" was all about. For over two months preceding the wedding, a different family was invited to visit each night, bringing the wedding gifts and "seeing the bedroom." It was an Italian wedding custom for the family to prepare the bedroom with the finest items they could find anywhere in the world. The newlyweds would stay in it the first night of their honeymoon, but they were not permitted to see it until then. By that time the room had been completely transformed. It was a show place, fit for a King and Queen – all new furniture, bed, dressers, tables, lamps, imported drapes, bedding, rugs, and special wall coverings.

It was such a grand and remarkable wedding that **Jo** and I couldn't help but have a marvelous time. We met a lot of fun-loving, enjoyable people. The young men we had seen the night we had arrived were mostly relatives or good friends living on that block. They had a special place for us to park, even that first night, if we had bothered to stop. The reception was out of this world, too, with an orchestra, beautiful music, and flash bulbs everywhere. These amazing people knew how to prepare a wedding. It was well over 24 hours of joy and excitement and sheer pleasure. A large group even accompanied the newlyweds to the train station the next day to see them off on the honeymoon. The honeymoon was to be in Sun Valley and the newlyweds were given a large sum of money to do with as they pleased.

We headed on to New York City with a couple of other out-of-towners who tried to help us find Blanche. We tried, but to find a specific Smith in New York City was a losing proposition. We never found her. I believe she was living with her daughter and still making people ecstatic with the joy she always gave. Her work was remarkable and each person who knew her was enriched. She once wrote a note on a Christmas card that God had given her me to be with when she couldn't be with her daughter. God works in mysterious ways for those who believe. We couldn't find Blanche in New York, but I know **Jo** and I will find her in Heaven.. Returning home, we brought all the happy memories with us.

Each Christmas for the next several years, we exchanged Christmas cards with the Panichelli's. They had four children and Joe became a successful lawyer. Eventually we drifted apart due to the distance between us and the letters stopped coming. Joe was a fine man and I'll try to look him up in Heaven; maybe we can relive the wedding and all the good times we had. When you think back, you realize that the good things on earth flash by too fast. You don't have the time any more to enjoy and savor the pleasures of life. I'm sure God has a better plan for us in Heaven.

We started this adventure out with a
fright
that soon disappeared and turned into delight
Attending this wedding with Jo at my side
was joy to see our best man caressing his bride
The greeting they gave us was awesome from
the start
Joe, friends, and family added joy to our hearts
Jo and I found out that a first impression
is sometimes meant to teach us a lesson
Jo knew so much more that I
angels view objects high in the sky
When Jo and I are back together
the view I will see will be much better
Jo being next to me is all I ask
being without her will have passed
When I tell her I missed and love her so much
she'll softly say, "Aw, Ken, now you hush"
***Oh!** what a **glorious** day I'm looking for*
*being with **Jo**, the one **I love** and **adore**.*

Girl of our Dreams

I felt I was predestined to recognize the girl that I would want to be with forever. I had an image imprinted in my mind. When I first saw **Jo**, the fit was uncanny. My Mother and Dad asked me if we all could have loved **Jo** before we met her. Girl of our dreams – is that possible? I think it could have been so.

I know Mother was capable of having dreamt ***Jo*** *up for me, her only child, but Dad had to meet* ***Jo*** *in order to come to love her. God, too, had to have had a hand in it. My belief that* ***Jo*** *was my angel supports this. Never a harsh word between us, no disagreements, finding nothing wrong with one another. When your expectations are exceeded over and over again, what more could one wish for? I will ask God how much love one man can have for the one love of his life? I wonder if it's proper to ask God? If not God, whom would I ask?*

Jo *was the girl I honored with the sacred wedding vows we both knew we would never break.* ***Jo*** *would never say anything she didn't believe. She always had a great love for her church and the desire to live as she felt God wanted her to.*

As each year passed, my caring love for ***Jo*** *grew. I can't speak for her, but I know how I felt. All that my eyes could take in, holding her in my arms for hours, being next to her always adding love, and hearing her voice only increased that. Never lustful or in a rush, just smooth, slow, steady happiness, always very satisfying. I started out with a great deal of love for* ***Jo*** *and thinking of her only increased my love for her. I know I set a personal best record with my love for* ***Jo****.*

I have painted myself into that writer's corner again. I do know it's proper to pray, so I pray that I spend eternity with ***Jo****. She had an all-consuming passion for everything she loved; I have the same for her, I always will. Our new life together in Heaven will renew that passion, that bliss, that* ***Jo*** *and I felt so many times. Until then, I will continue to read all the stories about our wonderful life together here in this world and contemplate the future always, "Remembering* ***Jo****, the girl of my dreams."*

Dell and Chuck

Jo and I met Dell Mercer through our brother-in-law Chuck. They went to mechanics school together after Chuck got out of the Navy. Dell was a lot of fun and **Jo** and I enjoyed a lifetime relationship with him. He was what I would call "boat crazy." Everything he did was around and about boats.

Dell's father was a life-long Ford employee and so was Dell; the Mercers were a nice family and very generous to Dell's friends. They owned a lot on one of the Long Lakes, allowing Dell and his friends to have it on weekends. Air-conditioning wasn't in our price range, so the lakes were the place to be in the summertime. The lot had a few things that drew us close together – a bar-b-cue, a picnic bench on a concrete slab, a small tool-locker, and a privy. All this was in the woods, so it had to rain very hard to force us home. A sod farm was nearby and we would play baseball, volleyball or any other game we wanted on this turf; nothing hurt it.

The women would drive one of the cars down to the beach, because it was a long walk from the property. One sunny summer day, the women had been swimming, but had gotten out and toweled off. They decided to return to the lot for lunch, but Bob was still wet from swimming, so he got in the trunk; he was not visible, as he held the lid slightly open, so he could get some air. Some young guys, seeing these four beautiful girls driving in a convertible, pulled up next to them and tried to start a conversation. When the girls wouldn't respond to their attentions, they resorted to forcing them off the road. Just then the trunk opened and Bob, a good-sized muscular, young man, emerged; the surprised and frightened would-be suitors left in a big hurry leaving Bob and the girls with a great story to tell over lunch.

It was a magnificent day for all of us down on the beach near the water. We loved seeing our wives and girlfriends enjoying themselves sunning and swimming in their colorful bathing suits. All of the women were so beautiful and all of us men were so proud of them. The women I remember most were Jo, Irene, Marge, and Mary. Dell had not met Connie, his future wife, yet. We had some friends that would come and go, but the four best friends are the ones we have a lot of photographs of and the ones we remember still. We enjoyed the swimming, the food, and the cool weather in the evening, and the nearby town we drove into if we needed anything. We had such fun in the sun, creating future memories, planning more fun things to do together, and then heading home in the moonlight.

Dell had been working on a speedboat for at least two years and it seemed like forever, but during that summer the launching date was quickly approaching. Dell had billed this day as the greatest day of his young life. Chuck and Dell, who were the best of friends because of their shared love of the water, had tested the oversize Evinrude engine many

times. Jo and I had stopped by several times to monitor their progress; the boat was looking really great. It was a white speedboat, but if Dell wanted to take extra passengers all he had to do was take off a hatch. Our anticipation for the launching was building.

It was a beautiful summer day when Dell finally launched his boat. All our friends had gathered to see this and take a ride in his wonderful work of art. We had to walk out to the end of a long wooden ramp with rowboats tied on both sides to get into the boat. Dell had connected the outboard motor to a steering wheel and the throttle cut-off control panel. With only Chuck and Dell in the speedboat, it rode high in the water at full throttle. When the throttle was cut, the boat would drop into the water and stop in a very short distance. Chuck was stationed in a crouch position at the very nose of the boat hanging onto a metal handle to stop the boat from touching the ramp, thus preventing it from being scratched. Dell took great pride in doing this time and time again with great success and showmanship.

The men had taken several people out for rides and things were going great. Everybody was happy, waving and shouting fun things to one another. Then Chuck and Dell went out by themselves, Chuck at the nose in his crouched position. Dell was pushing the throttle wide open to show the high speed they could achieve. We were all lining up for another ride when Dell, racing for the ramp, hit the cut-off switch and it failed! He made a hard left turn and the boat leaped clear out of the water. This beautiful work of art, crashing into the dock, sent Chuck flying through the air from the sudden smash, looking thunderstruck. He did a complete somersault and landed on his feet in a row boat. The women were screaming and running to get out of the way of the flying boat before it smashed into them.

It happened so fast, no one got a photograph. What lives on is only what we saw and what we can remember. The boat had a huge gash in the side from crashing into the dock and immediately started to sink, but neither Chuck nor Dell had a scratch. They could have been killed or seriously injured; some of us, too. Surely God was with us that day. The boat had sunk in four foot of water, so we got it out easily enough. Dell took it home, repaired it, and had it back in the water the next day. We all talked about this for many years to come.

Several years later, Dell met Connie, the girl he married. **Jo** and I took a long trip on a larger boat they later owned with Dell and Connie and their five children. Their dog was with us, too. Dell, like his father before him, worked at Ford Motor Company for nearly 30 years before retiring. He became a Commander at the Ford Yacht Club where he attended a lot of special functions, all related to boats. Connie was the right girl for boating; their children grew up on the boats they owned. **Jo** and I relived these fond memories throughout our years together. It was always such a pleasure to share warm memories with my **Jo**.

Bob and Marge

Jo and I always figured that Bob and his wife, Marge, were our best friends. We double-dated a lot when we were all in our early twenties. They called us up on the phone the most, including us in their plans more than anyone else. We enjoyed being together and talking over our plans for the future.

Bob was a very hard worker, doing construction work mostly. He poured concrete for huge driveways and miles-long runways for airplanes. One time I saw him and his partner, Doug, at one of the factories where I was working. They both worked hard and did a wonderful job.

Bob was a big eater, sometimes ordering two meals for himself. He was a big consumer of alcohol, too, but I never saw it effect him. He stood 5 foot 11 inches and weighed 175 lbs and was very strong from the physical nature of his job. Marge was very pretty and you could tell she loved her man. She had beautiful white teeth and was an excellent swimmer. **Jo** and Marge got along famously; they were even about the same size and shape. They looked beautiful standing side by side. Bob and I were always very proud of them.

Bob was the friend who said, " order me one, too." when I was telling him that I was ordering a new Plymouth convertible. We both agreed they were the best cars we ever owned. Ours was white and his was red. In those days you ordered the Standard, the Deluxe, or the Special Deluxe model. We both ordered the best and got the best. We had so much fun, and so little trouble, with those two convertibles. The manufacturer only gave you a ninety-day warrantee, so you quickly searched out anything that was wrong with the car, but neither Bob nor I could ever find a thing wrong with our convertibles. Each time our wives would talk on the phone, I would break in and ask Bob about his car. He always said he couldn't find any thing wrong – " a convertible, and not even a rattle," he'd say. I had the same answer for him, too. "Good experiences shared," **Jo** always said, " can improve any friendship."

Bob worked long hours and made great money, but I think he might have been an over-spender. I didn't know all the particulars about his situation, but I don't believe he ever saved much for the future. It turned out that he didn't need it, because he died young and tragically.

The company he and his partner worked for sent them to Texas to learn how to put in a new product, a flooring material similar to concrete. His partner, Doug, said he didn't like working with, or being around it, but Bob thought it was okay. Shortly thereafter Bob got very sick and died, suffering a lot before he went. Doug believed too much handling of the new product brought on the illness, so he refused to work with it. Marge couldn't talk about Bob's death; she loved him so and missed him terribly. **Jo** and I tried to comfort her the best we could, but she couldn't participate in life now that Bob was no longer a part of it. Losing your beloved spouse is such a hard blow. Now I know just how she felt.

Jo and I never had a chance to really tell Bob and Marge how we felt about them. Youth is not the time, because you don't believe the good times could ever come to an end. I'm telling them now by writing about the joy that they gave us. We hope to be double-dating with them again, maybe riding the streets of heaven in those great convertibles. They were a wonderful couple and we always enjoyed calling them our best friends. We will always remember them and the good times we had together.

Marge

Bob

Marge & Bob

Marge and Bob our best young friends
so sorry in youth it had to end
Bob so friendly so strong in many ways
gone from us in so few days
Marge his true love, he was so proud,
telling me in secret, never out loud
When you're young, you keep things hidden
they will get out
there are other ways to show love,
no need to shout
Bob and I showed our love to Marge and Jo
our eyes, our words, our caresses
Being so happy, no need for guesses
Marge and Bob we will meet someday
Pent-up love will be displayed
Bob always drove setting sideways
glancing at Marge most of the way
Funny the small things you remember
of such a wonderful friend
It was his desire to see his love
from the beginning to the end.

Ruth and Bill

When Mother and Dad purchased their new home on Edmore, **Jo** and I moved in with them. We spent almost twenty years living there. Across the street there lived a wonderful couple named Ruth and Bill Ede. Ruth was very kind and a lovely person. **Jo**, most summer days, would cross the street and set on the porch talking with Ruth. **Jo** felt blessed knowing her. If **Jo** or I needed an answer to any question, it was in our library, "Bill Ede." Bill had the answer to anything and everything, but you had to pull it out of him. The answer was stored away; he tried to pretend it wasn't, but everyone knew it was. He would never brag or boast of his knowledge; in fact he gave the answer to you with so much ease, it raised the question in your mind as to how he was able to stockpile such a vast wealth of knowledge.

One Christmas season, **Jo** told me to buy whatever gift I wanted for myself. I shopped for, and eventually bought, an economical, three-quarter-size pool table. We didn't have much money to spend, but I felt *satisfied with what I had purchased. Ruth was unfortunate in having me as her partner one night when we four decided to play pool. Bill showed* ***Jo*** *how to hold the pool cue and the correct spot to hit the ball; being a perfectionist, and with Bill's instruction, the greatest pool player in the world wouldn't have had a chance that night against* ***Jo****. She was so happy to learn that she had the makings to be a pool shark. Ruth was stuck with me, but her Bill was outstanding. If she had had him as her partner,* ***Jo*** *and I wouldn't have stood a chance.*

Other times the four of us got together to play cards. ***Jo*** *and I were at their kitchen table one evening when Kevin, their youngest son, who had been asleep, woke up and wandered into the kitchen. Ruth picked him up, sat him on her lap, and we continued our game. Then he sleepily said he wanted a taste of his dad's beer. Bill got him a very small shot glass and poured in a small amount. Kevin drank a bit and quietly observed the adults for some time. He became restless and began talking, so Bill said to his little tot, "Drink your beer and go to bed." Kevin immediately did as his father had commanded. He drank his beer down in one gulp like any trooper, slammed his glass on the table, and then ran to his bed. We all broke out laughing as soon as Kevin was out of sight.*

When Bill and Ruth celebrated their 50th wedding anniversary, ***Jo*** *and I were honored to be able to attend. It was a wonderful party and we couldn't stop talking to our old friends.* ***Jo*** *and I had remarkable times on this earth because of these neighbors. Bill's trademark was a tasteful joke as he and Ruth were leaving any gathering. We hope Ruth and Bill will live across the street from us in heaven like in the good old days.* ***Jo*** *and I will look forward to that simple pleasure in the days to come.*

Little Brother

Johnny, my Mother's younger brother, had a fun – loving personality. You always enjoyed yourself when he was around. Johnny was always able to drink a lot and never show it. "Little brother" was what his sisters always called him, but he grew up to be a big man, tall, and a bit on the chunky side. It was odd that he had very small feet, size six and a half, for a man six-foot.

He always had a nice car, nice clothes, and was admired by all who knew him. He was an excellent dancer. My Mother, dancing with Johnny, could take over the dance floor. In later years, **Jo** and Johnny danced together and he knew she was something special.

Dad got Johnny a job at Chrysler; he had been working at the used car lot and was very proficient. He had two jobs, money pouring in; the Depression was over and all was right with the world. The war started and Chrysler was working overtime. My dad had to close his used car lot, but "little brother" had more than enough to do with the defense work.

Uncle Bert and Johnny palled around together and there was never any trouble. One day Bert and Johnny, with four other friends who were out partying together, went down to enlist in the service. All of the men were accepted, but Johnny; he had broken his ankle in a car accident some years before and was rejected. This was always a big joke with the rest of the family – Johnny staying home and Bert going, leaving a wife and child and a solid defense job behind. Johnny was the cause of Bert enlisting, yet they remained good friends, the war having ended without any of our family members being seriously hurt. We were a blessed family even during the depression and the war years.

Bert was away in the Navy while his wife, Daisy, worked for Chrysler. Dad had gotten her the job. Everybody was so happy when the war was suddenly over. With the soldiers returning, things started to get back to normal. Then it happened – "little brother" took a wrong turn in the road. A friend of his mother owned a catering business and on the weekends he would work for her at local parties and weddings. It started out just fine and lasted for a long time, but attending party after party began to cause trouble for "Little brother." He began making some very poor decisions. The drinks began to affect him like they hadn't when he was younger. He married and divorced one young girl after another. He provided the money to raise his children, but no time or love was given to them. It was a disaster for the wives and children. Thank God, my mother did not live to see this. Alcohol was his downfall; he suffered, as did his children, his wives, and the world. A wonderful, joyous, fun-loving personality all wasted. Jo and my Dad tried to help out at different times, but Johnny wouldn't, couldn't, follow through.

Everyone loved that little boy
he was so full of life and joy
What a wonderful life he would have had
if his choice had been the good over the bad
Had a future that would last
what he did was take the wrong path
Little brother was liked by all
until the wrong path caused his fall
What he did to his family, oh, what despair
partying, drinking, he just didn't care.

Jo was my Angel

In my attempt to become a good writer, I often had to consult my dictionary. I looked up the definition of an angel and it read: " an angel is superior to man." **Jo** was certainly superior to me and spiritual as well. I know she was my guardian. Her love of white and the desire for everything to be so clean – even dirt – should have told me long ago that she was an angel.

How would you feel if you had been living with an angel most of your life? My Mother loved Dad, **Jo** and I so much, I believe she asked God to make **Jo** an angel. Mother being such a wonderful person while here on earth, God granted her that wish. After all, **Jo** was the perfect candidate.

If I looked in a mirror through **Jo's** eyes, I would see the beauty she saw every day. I don't know how she functioned thinking of herself as just a lady – **Jo** had to know she was extraordinary to do the things she did. I was never as kind as she was; I tried so hard, but couldn't. The soft voice she could produce for me, I tried to produce for her, but couldn't reach the levels she so easily achieved.

She must have become an angel over a period of time, because I don't think God told her. If God had told her, she would have known and told me, because she never kept any secrets from me. We went to two different Halloween Parties and **Jo** dressed up as, yes, an Angel. That thick flowing brown, gleaming, wavy, beautiful hair around a face that was smooth and soft with a smile so sincere, what more could I ask for in a portrait? I think I have just described an angel; **Jo** was certainly that for me. Look for a Guardian Angel for yourself and have a lifetime of joy as I did. The only people I told about my great love for **Jo** was Mother and Dad, but this book is meant to tell the whole world.

How do you judge a person here on Earth? Usually from the way they treat you and what you know about them. The more time you spend with them, the better chance your judgment will be correct. Loving **Jo** does bias my judgment of her, but still my judgment is correct – she was my angel. When I calculated the time I was with **Jo**, years, months, days, hours, and seconds it was more than any other person on Earth. I will always give thanks to God, for the blessing he bestowed on me – my time here on earth with my wonderful **Jo**.

One Saturday, **Jo** had gone shopping alone. We had only been in our new home a few months when the chimes sounded. I looked out to see a group of young girls at our front door. I opened the door and asked if I could help them. They told me that a Mrs. America had moved into the neighborhood and they were sure it was **Jo**. They had seen her come out of this house; she had to be Mrs. America. They said, "you sure have a beautiful wife." I told them that she wasn't crowned, but she sure was Mrs. America to me. When **Jo** came home

I rushed to tell her. She laughed and said, "those silly girls need their eyes examined." If that was true, then I needed to have mine examined, too. The first day I saw ***Jo****, I knew that many others would see the beauty I saw.*

I have been writing about ***Jo*** *for several months now. It's easy to write nice things about her, but I repeat myself too many times – how much I love her and miss her so. I know I'd even defend the bad things about* ***Jo****, if I could think of any. Would my angel have a need to be defended? I'm sure she wouldn't. In all my stories she's always revered. If I said to* ***Jo****, "I heard this cute joke today, but it's a little racy," without hesitation, she would walk away and find something else to do. I would never force anything on* ***Jo****, because I wanted her to be happy. If it did not please* ***Jo****, it didn't please me. She, too, always took my feelings into consideration, always wanting me to be happy. I admit I had bad days; I was human and let people know it.* ***Jo*** *would gently ask me, "aren't you feeling well?" She could sense my feelings sometimes before I could. We both used maybe 5 aspirin a year, nothing else. If* ***Jo*** *was ever sick, you would seldom know; my angel was not a complainer.*

I knew if anything bad happened, ***Jo*** *had no part in it, down to the smallest particle. I remember her being very upset once when an untruth was told about her. She had learned that someone was saying she had said somethung she hadn't.* ***Jo*** *went straight to her friend, to set the record straight, but her friend still wouldn't believe her. Her love of the truth was always present; she wanted to be vindicated. That was very important to her. If* ***Jo's*** *friend knew her as I had, she would have known that* ***Jo*** *was telling the truth.*

One evening a program was on television that I wanted to watch. ***Jo*** *wasn't interested in it, so she worked very hard at other things. All* evening she was busy while I hadn't even moved out of my armchair. She must have done 20 different things, showered and had already gone to bed when I entered the bedroom. I knew she wasn't asleep, so I got in bed and left the light on even though the switch is on my side. Some time passed before **Jo** quietly said, "Ken, aren't you going to turn off the light?" I quickly flipped the covers back and in a mock harsh voice said, "do I have to do everything?" It seemed like a long time passed, then she said, "Aw, Ken," with a little laugh. She had figured out I was joking with her, that I wanted her to know I appreciated all she had done, while I had done nothing but watch my program. I turned out the light and hugged my wonderful wife, my angel **Jo**.

Jo was always up early, always looking forward to each new day. The house was clean, nothing out of place. She would put on a jacket to go out, not much to change in the closet, but she would make a slight adjustment. She would take off her slippers, then adjust her shoes sitting in the closet. My angel was always making a final touch as she moved through life, never leaving anything undone. Big changes are seldom necessary when you're an angel every day.

The stories over the years I was with her all point to her being an Angel – my parents thinking they had loved her before, so many people drawn to her, her wanting everything so clean and neat. Even the language she used to express herself was gentile, never a swear word. She was always making dark places light, never being upset with me, and anticipating everyone's wishes. Her loving life so much and vocalizing it to me so many times, having and giving so much love, the way she dressed for Church to visit God, and her unending kindness. Some people have a few of the good traits, but **Jo's** were endless to me. She was always amazing me with more and more.

*Jo checked her slip constantly, made sure her jewelry was sparkling. In the rain she checked to see that her rain gear was doing the job it was designed for. Did she have a run in her silk hose? Was her makeup smeared? Was her car clean? She made sure she wasn't late for an appointment. She took care of old things as if they were new. All fair-minded humans might think this was excessive, but you must remember: **Jo** was an angel. **Jo** was always on her way to Heaven. Anything she did was special. When she hung out a wash, you knew it was her wash, because the whites were a little whiter. When you see a picture of angels, aren't they whiter than white?*

*Jo had a contagious composure with me – so calm, quiet, peaceful, and kind – what a love it was. When I miss her, I think of her portrait. **Jo** was my cameo of life. Her memories are everywhere. When I think of a cameo it is from before our time, but it is real. Her model lives on in my mind. I can't change that and don't want to. How could she embrace so much? My life with **Jo** confirmed what I must have guessed when I first saw her. She was the only one to take me to a better place with love along the way. You know it is my wish to be in Heaven with Mother, Dad and **Jo** as quickly as possible. When God created **Jo** for me, and made her an angel as my Mother requested, that was my **Jo** forever.*

When
I saw Jo that first day
I knew I couldn't stay away
She had a charm so strong
to leave her would be wrong
I wanted to protect her
never to neglect her
Joy, love and kindness did abound
whenever my Angel Jo was around
Mother asked God to make Jo an Angel
the perfect candidate
Mother Dad and Jo are now in heaven
I don't want to wait
That smile she always took to bed
I never knew of her to shed
I keep knocking at her door
She's in heaven forevermore
Love was always with my Jo all of her life
She shared it with me as my angel wife
Jo, my Angel here on earth,
had to enter heaven first
So I could write about our life
having Angel Jo for my wife
God wanting everyone on earth to know
by reading the book, "Remember My Jo."

My Beautiful Jo

Jo wanted everything soft and clean. The time she spent with my mother was very satisfying for both of them. They learned about taking care of themselves- hair, skin, eyes, complexions, cold cream for your face; hand and body lotions, they talked for hours on each subject. I said **Jo** and Leta were cut from the same cloth. They would look at magazine pictures of hairstyles and fancy clothing like two children in a candy shop. It was so wonderful to be a part of the years they had together.

I can't remember **Jo** stepping out of the house without making sure she felt she was presentable. When the bell rang or there was a knock at the door, I had to answer it unless **Jo** felt she was looking very nice. I always answered the door, because it was **Jo's** wish and I always wanted to honor her wishes. While I answered the door **Jo** would rush to correct any flaw she thought she might have, then present herself as soon as she could in a good light. If I were away from the house, **Jo** would be in readiness to answer the door. She never wanted any one to see her not looking her best. I always made a joke that **Jo** would want to be dressed up for a burglar.

It was always a delight to be around her. She did her nails twice a week while watching television. Her skin was so nice and soft to be next to. She smelled so good because "Estee Lauder" was the right mix for her. How **Jo** could do so much and never neglect herself and anyone around her, I will never know. She had a pleasing heart and soul for everyone. I try to figure out why **Jo** left before me, but I can only think that Almighty needed my angel. That is what **Jo** was to me, an angel.

Jo Was Sensitive

Jo was a very sensitive individual. Things that didn't matter to some people meant a lot to **Jo**. Saying something rude or uncaring could upset her very much. **Jo** and I had respect for our families, our friends, and the people we associated with. We would overlook small infractions, but we did have our limits.

Jo liked good times, but nothing loud or vulgar. She had thin skin and she didn't want to be hurt or see anybody else hurt. **Jo** wanted to honor the position a person had.

Excess of anything she shunned, she didn't like waste, overspending was as bad as saving too much. She was overjoyed when good things happened. A complement was worth 100 put-downs. Kind, gentle, sweet was my astonishing **Jo**. I'm obsessed with her memories, rightfully so. **Jo** was my life and I want to be with her. Writing about **Jo** is a way of my being near her. **Jo** had some hard knocks but she weathered them as good as any mortal could. I didn't know what she was thinking, but I had faith that it would work out and be virtuous. **Jo** never brought any baggage you had to carry. Her luggage was light if you insisted on helping her.

Jo liked music and dancing. We took dancing lessons from a good teacher, but **Jo** was a lot better than I was. For some reason, I just couldn't quite get it right. Our instructor could do great things with **Jo**, but I just couldn't take over like he could. I think I loved **Jo** too much and, consequently, tried too hard. It was hard for me to direct my Angel.

Jo had a good feeling for music. She could hear an artist for the first time and say he or she will be famous eventually. I never knew her to be wrong. Glen Miller, Sinatra, Elvis, Cole, and then she moved into

Reba, Judds, and Travis. ***Jo*** *liked love songs, slow, elegant music. If the music got loud, she didn't want to hear it. We both liked Willie Nelson's "Georgia on My Mind."*

I hope that ***Jo*** *likes the music in Heaven and that in Heaven I can be a good dancer with my remarkable* ***Jo****. It's what I'm looking for.*

Jo never made fun
of anyone
she felt that was very sad
She wanted love, nothing bad
I always went before her
to clear the way
Testing the water
for that day
She sensed what I was doing
I heard her say,
"Our love will last and always grow."
Another reason to remember my Jo.

Jo and Chrysler

*We both spent most of our lives working, as most of us do. I first met **Jo** when she was working at an ice cream parlor. It was love at first sight; I **liked** ice cream, but I **loved Jo**. Walking into that parlor was the best step I ever took. When I saw **Jo**, I said to myself, "If I could only be good enough for this beautiful young girl!" I couldn't stop coming back to see her.*

*I must have done something right because we did start going together. I remember taking her home from work. I was always looking forward to the workday ending, so I could take her home. Many years later, I would joke about how her girlfriend Jean always gave me bigger dips of ice cream, but **Jo** was the only girl for me. **Jo** soon had a job at the Broadway Capital, a movie theatre downtown. I began picking her up very late at night when she got off work to drive her home.*

***Jo** was still working there and going to high school when I entered the Service Training to become a pilot in the Army Air Force. It* wasn't too long before she graduated and got a job in the office at Kresge's. With the war on, she soon secured a job in the war effort and moved in with my parents so she could ride with Dad

to work. **Jo** ended up working for my Dad for some time. They liked each other very much in a very short time. What was not to like; they were both very special people.

After I returned from my wartime service and we had gotten married, I sometimes worked on a different shift than **Jo**. She would adjust to the change, but most of the time we worked nearly the same hours. I usually began work before **Jo** and she did more than her share because of it. **Jo** was up first and got breakfast on the table let the dog out, and packed my lunch. She had laid out her clothes the night before.

After I left, she would put the dishes away and clean up then leave for work. On my return home nothing was ever out of place. **Jo** would drive 15 miles to work – not an easy job on the streets she had to travel. **Jo** would get in the groceries and do any other shopping that

Newspaper Clipping

1965 – Detroit: A blizzard kills at least 27 people – 21 fatal heart attacks and six traffic deaths – and dumps more than 11 inches of snow on the city and suburbs. At least 50,000 cars became stuck in the deep snow banks.

*needed to be done. She always bought ice cream, because we still liked it after all these years. I would volunteer to help, but she said, "Thanks, but I'll do it." I had work to do around the house, but it was never as much as **Jo** did.*

***Jo** worked for Chrysler for nearly 30 years. A lot of good years with mostly very good people. She had many men and women friends at Chrysler. I talked to a lot of them over the years that told me what a lucky man I was.*

*One winter morning we woke up to a very heavy snowfall. The radio announcers said to stay home unless you had an emergency. I told **Jo** I was not going to work. **Jo** told me of an important meeting scheduled for that day. Her boss would want her in. I didn't want her to go, but she insisted. "I'll clear the snow around the house, and wait for your phone call," I said. I would be ready to go to **Jo's** aid if she needed me. It was the only way I would let her go.*

*It took **Jo** over three hours to make that thirty minute drive. She called from work and told me she was coming home. Only a few had shown up, so everyone was being sent home. It was cold and snow was still falling, but much lighter now.*

*I helped people in the neighborhood as I watched for **Jo** to return. Cars were stuck, broken down, and lined up because some other cars had spun out. It was one of the worst days we had ever had. I looked up*

*and **Jo** was driving past cars that couldn't move; she slid around the corner and into our drive, putting the car in the garage like any normal day. She had been on the road for over seven hours and was still smiling.*

*She felt her boss and Chrysler needed her that day and when **Jo** thought she was needed she had to try. She was loyal from the bottom of her tiny shoes to the top of her dazzling hair. I will always be loyal to my amazing, gorgeous **Jo**. I know she will be loyal to me. We belong together forever.* **Remember my Jo** *and what she would do if she thought she was needed.*

*Mother Nature was no match for my **Jo** that day. The effort **Jo** would make always amazed me. I can never say enough good things about **Jo**. So many times she would do almost the unattainable. After that record snowfall, it took a good week for things to get back to normal. She had done so well that day, but I was a nervous wreck worrying about my **Jo**.*

Jo worked for Chrysler for many a year
when profits were up, she was full of
good cheer
She looked forward to progress, any job
they assigned
perfection was always the goal on her mind
If she thought they needed her she would
be there
always doing much more than her share
behind the wheel, the weather couldn't stop
her true
love and devotion was driving Jo's Chrysler.

"Aw, Ken"

Jo had some favorite expressions and "aw, Ken" was one of them. She was so soft and gentle. If she didn't want to do something she might say, "Aw, Ken." If I said something out of the way, that old man, she would say "Aw, Ken," which meant I should have said elderly gentleman. When I agreed with her about her new Sebring, she said "Aw, Ken," with a little laugh that meant "I love you, Ken."

When I was shooting with my VCR camera the ladies always hide from it, but the dog steps up front. When I told **Jo** that, she said "aw, Ken," that meant I understand what you're saying. Sometimes it was a question. Other times it was a no, no. If it had a small laugh after the "Aw, Ken," it was I love you, Ken. We didn't want to be mushy in public, but **Jo** had her ways of letting me know. I would hear it maybe twice a month but it was always welcome, because it was so nice coming from **Jo**. When she said it, I had to put my thinking cap on and move into **Jo's** mind. It was always a pleasure to try to think what **Jo** was thinking. You knew that only good things, some treasure, was at the end of your journey. **Jo's** eyes and smile could talk to me, always with love.

When I look back, I realize that my world has to include **Jo**; when she was not in the picture, the picture couldn't be developed. With **Jo** around, I could enjoy everything - walk in the woods, run, play, sing, dance, look at the stars and look forward to each moment. Without **Jo**, I can't enjoy anything. I have been told that in Heaven I will have an eternal embrace with my **Jo**, I want that now, this second. Embracing **Jo** for eternity is all I wish for.

If I could hear **Jo** say "Aw, Ken," one more time while I'm here on earth, it would be a miracle. I wish God would allow me to see **Jo** and hear her voice one more time while I'm here on earth. I celebrated *every day waking up next to* ***Jo****. Please let me have that celebration again.*

You know how I loved
her voice
hoping, "Aw, Ken," was
her choice
Jo's secret phrase
mostly given in praise
Jo's love secretly passed
"Aw, Ken," with a little
laugh

City Slicker

On a beautiful, sunny morning in October, we started out for our Florida vacation. It would be two weeks of joy and nothing could spoil what we had planned. I was driving our brand new car and **Jo** was my co-pilot and navigator. I was looking forward to sun and heat during the day and night life and shows during the evenings and the pleasure of being with **Jo**. **Jo** in her bathing suit lying in the sand near the pool would be a wonderful sight to behold. First, we had to get to Miami. We had had our breakfast and were several hours into our trip moving along as smooth as silk, nearing the top of a hill, when out of the blue, our new car shut down. It's hard to control a car when you lose power to the steering and brakes; fear immediately set in, but we managed to coast off the roadway, coming to a gentle stop on the gravel shoulder.

We were now stranded on a little country road in Georgia. To the left of us was a driveway leading to a neat looking farmhouse. I said to **Jo**, "I'll call from that farmhouse," but just then a lady in a very large car began to pull out of the long drive. She saw we were in trouble, so she asked what she could do to help. "We need to get our car to a garage," I said. Being the Georgia peach she was, this lady said, "I will take you to a gas station-garage at the bottom of the hill and they will take the best care of you there. I will get you on your way as soon as

possible." It was still cool, so **Jo** *decided to stay with the car until I returned with help. The lady said, "we'll only be gone a short time." It was only a short ride to the bottom of the hill to the gas station, barn and small general store, all rolled into one; the store was newer than the barn, but not by much.*

The good lady quickly told them of our dilemma and arranged for a farm boy with an old truck to take me back to the car. The lady was a prominent person in the community, so the owners of the garage assured us that we would get good treatment as a result of her personal request. Returning to the car, I told **Jo** *that the gas station-barn and general store were in pretty bad shape, glumly adding, " we may spend our vacation at this location."* **Jo** *said, "Aw, Ken, everything will be just fine." The farm boy and I tried pouring a little gasoline in the carburetor to start the engine, but that didn't work, so he told me he would give me a good push to get me coasting down the hill. When I reached the barn-like garage, I was to roll in as far as possible. We started rolling down the hill at a pretty good clip and I could plainly see that the road and floor of the station was all dirt, but it was pitch black as we entered the old barn. I was trying my best to stop the car in total darkness. God was with us, because we stopped just five feet short of a heavy metal workbench. When they turned on the lights I saw that three 150-watt light bulbs, all dangling naked from extension cords, was the complete extent of the lighting system.*

The farm boy told us he would go get the mechanic. Our shiny new car looked so out of place in the dingy old barn. I saw a fenced-in, crib-

like area with belts and farm tractor parts hanging from the wooden beams. Parts from many trucks and cars were lying in disarray On the metal workbench I had just barely managed to escape colliding with. I began to sweat.

A wooden step led to a screen-door that opened upon the general store. **Jo** and I entered. When we asked for a bottle of pop, we were told they only had soda. It turned out to be the same thing. We sat down resignedly to drink our soda while waiting for the mechanic to show up. He was an elderly little farmer dressed in bib overalls and wearing very small, granny glasses. He said, "If you will kindly come with me, I'll take a look at it." "No parts department, poor lighting, junk parts all over the place, a little man that can hardly see," I thought, " Oh, boy, here we go, or maybe not."

"What kind of a car is this?" he asked. " It's a Dodge," I proudly said. "Who makes it?" "Chrysler Corporation." "Who? You had better wait in the store, while I see what I can do." I began to sweat even more. **Jo** took a seat and began chatting with a couple of young girls who had a lot of questions for a friendly, well-dressed city girl just passing through. **Jo** was laughing with them, her wonderful laugh,

but I was sweating more and more; I just couldn't control it. I was thinking of that elderly man out there with our new car and what he might be doing. I kept going to the screen-door to see if anything good was happening out in the barn. The mechanic came to the door and asked me if the car was a six or eight cylinder. I told him, "eight," as my heart sunk. I walked to **Jo** and excitedly said, "I can't believe this. When we get out of here, I'm heading for the first Chrysler dealer I can find. This mechanic can't know anything, if he's asking me if it's a six or an eight."

A short time later the mechanic called me out to the barn to start the car. He had his head under the hood while I tried the ignition a couple of times. It turned over, but still wouldn't start. He slammed the hood and walked toward me, saying he would go figure the bill. "What about my car?" I asked. "You can start it up, it's O. K. now," he said. He was right, it started up as if it was charmed. I backed it out, filled it with gas, paid a very small bill and we were happily on our way again in style. These strangers had been very helpful, kind, and enjoyable. A few miles down the road, **Jo** quietly asked if I was still planning to look for a Chrysler dealer. I turned to her and with a rueful smile said, "not when it's running this good."

Georgia remains one of our favorite States; I love the drawl they use when speaking. "You all come back now, ya hear?" was a favorite phrase and the song; "Georgia on my mind" was a favorite of ours, too. Talking with **Jo** about what had happened, we surmised that this elderly gentleman, as **Jo** would have called him, I would have called him a prankster, had spotted the problem – maybe a loose wire – from the start. Something very simple. He had some fun with this city slicker and his beautiful wife. This prankster had a good tale to tell his friends, for many years to come, how he had that young City Slicker sweating for some time over his sparkling new automobile. You know, we never had a bit more trouble with that car.

I did, however, have some trouble with the tropical sun once we made it to Florida. The sun hit me hard the first day; I had covered up all but my ankles and feet, but I got severely burned. I couldn't walk for a day, but ***Jo*** *tenderly nursed me back to health. At a parrot jungle we took a great picture of* ***Jo*** *with five parrots on her arms, head and shoulders. The trainer picked* ***Jo*** *out of this huge amphitheater and talked her into having one parrot placed on each of her arms. Once he had two on, she couldn't move, so he added three more. I always teased* ***Jo*** *about that. I'm tearing up now as I remember the great joy I had with my* ***Jo*** *in Miami.* ***Jo*** *looked so pretty on the Miami Beach. She retained that fresh Georgia-peach look all her life. The most fun was the nightlife and* ***Jo*** *looking so beautiful. My love for* ***Jo*** *under the Moon over Miami. I hope I will enjoy it in my next life, too.*

Finding Georgia living up to its warm and sunny reputation, I asked ***Jo*** *if we should stop for some ice cream. "Great idea," she responded, "stop at the next place you see." A few miles further, I saw a box-like building with posters all over the windows advertising just what we were craving.* ***Jo*** *told me what she wanted, but I couldn't make up my mind. Opening the little pass-through door, a very pretty young girl asked, "what can I get you-all?" I told her* ***Jo's*** *order and then asked, " do you have a Good Humor?" which was a brand of ice cream I was used to ordering in Michigan. She smiled a slow smile and said, "we all like to think we do." That got a big laugh from both* ***Jo*** *and me. Apparently, that ice cream was not known in the South at that time. I will never forget that young Georgia peach or the other wonderful people we made contact with on our memorable trip.*

Her sparkle in Miami
came as no surprise to me
Anyplace that Jo did go
everyone was sure to know
Parrot jungle charmed by Jo
picked her to enrich the show
Seeing her charm as I first did
sure that it should not be hid
The joy I had all my life
taking Jo for my wife.

Co-Pilot Navigator

Jo was my navigator through life and the best co-pilot I could have had. Her plan was to take you on a straight and sure flight to your destination, no matter the weather. We always planned for our journey to be together; now I'm lost and alone and keep asking for her guidance. The following story will show you how lost I can get.

One day while returning to Michigan from a Florida vacation, we were driving through Dayton, Ohio during rush hour. **Jo** had very seldom taken a nap or even closed her sparkling blue eyes during this long road trip, but we had run into a very heavy rainstorm and the sound of steady rain had enveloped the car, lulling her to sleep. She had marked the route beforehand that I was to take, so I knew the Interstate Highway that I was to follow for many miles. She was not neglecting her duty. **Jo** knew it would be a long time before our route number would change and she planned to be awake long before then to assist me, but the heavy rush-hour traffic had forced me into the far right lane, where I had to follow a harried traffic policeman's direction and make an unanticipated right hand turn.

Half a block down I turned right into an alley with the intention of making two more right turns to bring me back to my original route. I must have missed a sign in the heavy rain, because the alley had a roadblock in it forcing me to turn into a car wash. Once inside the

building, I had to wake ***Jo*** *up to get out of our car. We walked the length of the car wash, paid, and were once again on our way.* ***Jo*** *didn't question me or say a word. Out in the heavy rainstorm again I brought the subject up, asking if she didn't wonder why we were getting the car washed in a rainstorm? She said, " Aw, Ken, I knew you must of had a good reason." Only an Angel would have given that answer!*

I'm sure that when the time comes for God to file the final flight plan for me, he will send me my ***Jo****. She plotted the route for me here on earth and assisted me for all the years we were together. I'm lost without her and I know it. I need* ***Jo*** *as my Co- Pilot-Navigator to enter Heaven. What a glorious day that will be,* ***Jo*** *with me, flying together again.*

Life was such fun
when we were one
Not only my wife
Jo was my life
Should I go on
the past is gone
Without a voice
I have no choice
With Jo as my Navigator
I worried no more
I can only pray
till judgment day
That Jo will come
to fly me away
I can't think of a flight
with more delight
From beginning to end
***Jo and Ken**.*

Jo and Stocks

We moved into our new home. We had been preparing for this day for several years. The counter we would eat at was large enough for a television. I stopped and picked up a color model, the first one we had, black and white until then. When we had the T.V. for a short time, I realized it wasn't a good place to view it. I stopped and picked up a stand to set it on, thinking of putting it in the family room. It looked too small for that room, another mistake of mine. I called **Jo** in and she said, "We need a big set." When you move into a new home you are overwhelmed by the cost and I felt we were tapped out, so I said, "**Jo**, if you want a big set, we will have to make some money real quick."

"How do we do that?" she asked.

"You pick a good stock that moves up fast and we get the big set."

"Let's try," **Jo** said.

" You try, **Jo**, I'm not doing well in stocks at this time."

"What kind of a set is that you just bought?"

"RCA," I answered.

" I like that, buy some shares in that company."

"**Jo**, just call the broker in the morning and have the stock put it in your name," I said, thinking this would stall her for a while. She didn't delay, however; she called the next morning and purchased the shares in her name. A wild rumor came out, the stock shot up, and **Jo** sold it, bought her big set and still had more money than she had invested. When I inquired how she had accomplished this, she simply replied, "Aw, Ken." The rumor wasn't true; the stock went back down. This was another time that **Jo** stepped in and saved the day.

*Once I took **Jo** in as a real partner in the stock market, we never had another financial crisis. **Jo** always wanted to be loyal to her employer, Chrysler Corporation, so she always bought all the Chrysler stock she was allowed. We, also, bought Chrysler stock on our own and we always bought new Chrysler cars, fifteen in all.*

Dad's Pact

It was a tremendous shock to all of us when Mother suddenly passed away. It was totally unexpected and devastated us; however, it made us think more carefully of our own health and the health of our loved ones. **Jo** had been helping my mother weigh Dad's food, prepare his lunch, get his meals on time and watch him around meal time, so now she stepped in like an angel and began doing it full-time. All three of us were working for Chrysler. **Jo** was a secretary, Dad was a shift supervisor, and I was a pyrometer technician. One day Dad said, "the three of us must make a pact. If any one of us is in the hospital and wants out, the other two will agree to honor that wish at any cost." We all agreed.

A few years passed and Dad remarried, moving a few miles away, but I still saw him every day at work. One day he said, "tell **Jo** I'm going in the hospital to try a new medicine called DBI. My doctor thinks it might help me." Then he reminded me of our three-way pact. The first couple of days that Dad was in the hospital were fine, but by the third day he was in a coma. We were frantic with worry. When he came out of the coma, the first thing he said was, "get me out of this hospital and home now." I told the doctor that Dad was going home, even if I had to get a court order and the police. The doctor saw I was serious, so he signed the discharge papers and Dad came home that day. A couple of days later he went back to work, believing all the while that DBI hadn't worked for him.

Jo had liked a couple of nurses at the hospital who had been especially good to Dad and since she believed in rewarding kindness, she wanted to take them flowers. We went back to the hospital and gave them the flowers saying, "Dad is doing fine now, he's even back to work." One nurse took us aside and quietly told us that our checking

Dad out of the hospital as quickly as we had had caused them to more carefully monitor the other diabetic patients scattered throughout that floor. They were all doing poorly. They found out that the daily meals were having an adverse effect on them. This was quickly corrected and all were doing fine now. It was only **Jo's** wish to reward the nurse's kindness that enabled us to know the whole story.

Some years later, I was idling furnaces on the afternoon shift; Dad was on afternoons, too, since it was best for his diabetic condition. It was the late 50's and things were a little slow, so the plant was on a four-day operation. It was a big plant, so I had little time to visit with Dad. One afternoon I wasn't feeling too good, but rather than take the time to go find Dad, I went into the men's washroom to sit down. A few minutes later, one of my co-workers found me on the floor passed out cold. I had tossed up my lunch; everything was a mess.

Jo was at home when she received the call that I was being rushed to Ford Hospital. It was at the end of our shift, so she immediately called Dad. They both rushed to Ford Hospital where they were told I was doing well and that the doctors were trying to properly access my medical condition. **Jo** and Dad talked to the attending physician who wasn't sure what my problem was, but everyone agreed that I should stay overnight. **Jo** said, " I'll bring your shoes and clothes in the morning, dear," and tenderly gave me a kiss. I was still very sick, but **Jo** and Dad felt better knowing that when they left the hospital that night I was aware of what was going on.

They had been gone only a few minutes when a doctor I had never seen before came in and started to probe around my ribcage, asking what seemed to me to be crazy questions. When I told him how I felt, he wouldn't accept anything I said as the truth. I got angry and told him that I was going home. I called the nurse and told her, too. The doctor *said, "You'll have to sign papers to check yourself out. We can't be responsible for you." The hospital personnel were against my leaving, too, and said they couldn't provide transportation. I said," I'll sign your papers, just call me a cab." "But, Mr. Roberts," the night nurse said, "you don't have any clothes, shoes, or money." When I insisted that I was leaving regardless of clothes, shoes, or money, she called my home and* ***Jo*** *answered. I told her I was coming home and why, and then she asked to speak to the night nurse. She told her that she would pay for the cab, adding, "just send Ken home." The rain was pouring down as the cabby pulled up in our drive, but* ***Jo*** *was there waiting with the outside lights on. She was holding an umbrella, ready to help me into the house. My pajamas were laid out and the bed was turned down.* ***Jo*** *said she would sleep in the guest bedroom, so I could sleep in the next morning.*

The next morning ***Jo*** *was up early getting breakfast for Dad and quietly seeing him off to his Saturday morning Doctor's appointment. I slept till 10 A.M., and then she fixed me some soft-boiled eggs. By Monday morning I was back to normal and went to work that afternoon. I reported to the factory nurse who told me that I, along with five others, had had food poisoning from eating something tainted from the lunch wagon. The other guys were at home when they got sick, so we had all gone to different hospitals. That was the first time, and the last, that I ate anything from the lunch wagon!*

Meanwhile, Dad knew a woman who worked at Ford Hospital whom he asked to check my medical records. She found out that the doctor I hadn't trusted had scheduled me for an exploratory operation to find the cause of my pain. "Ken wouldn't have liked that," she said. "That's for sure," agreed Dad. Dad's pact all those years ago had worked beautifully for both of us with ***Jo*** *putting it in motion.*

Competition With Love

The minute I met **Jo** I wanted to be near her, wanted to please her. Things for us happened so fast that in a very few days, it seemed we had been together, and would be, forever. **Jo** had won me over, made me feel so good, so quick I didn't know what had happened. Just being around **Jo** was joy, without even having to say a word, but Mother and Dad said it best when they said they couldn't remember not loving **Jo**. Had the three of us loved her before we met her? She answered all our expectations, so I'd have to say yes.

I went to work and did my job, but when the workday was over and it was time to see **Jo** something special was about to happen. In the mornings you never had to wake me up to see **Jo**; I couldn't wait as the time grew near. Seeing her was such a joy – day or night, rain or shine, snow or sleet. I don't think even Webster contains the words that would tell what **Jo** means to me. Her smile was always special, her saying, "Aw, Ken," so welcome; her voice was slow and soft, never in a hurry. I was always so proud of her in our everyday life.

Jo would flit around the house, keeping everything so neat and clean. Nothing left undone, always spreading joy for the two of us. When I had some small plan that included her, it became an obsession; I had to complete what I thought would make her happy. Would **Jo** like it this way or would she like it better if I did it that way? Could she view it better if I put it there or there? I was always thinking about her, no matter what I was doing.

We had a Bill of Rights that helped us maintain the equality of our relationship. We each got, and gave, respect to each other. I never entered her domain without her permission. We knocked, never intruding; we were both shy and proud to be. We always asked *permission for anything that might embarrass the other … "Would you mind if I?" … "Could I see the book you're reading?" … "Could I see what you have written?" We felt we had no right to invade each other's privacy, but we shared in everything, if we felt it would make us both happier.* ***Jo*** *earned my love by putting me first in so many ways and I repaid her in kind. "I could have done that," she would say; "let me do that for you," I would say. I had to be near her, but I never wanted to crowd her. My desire now is to please God with what I write about* ***Jo****. I know that if I do it to the best of my ability, everyone that reads this book will* ***remember my Jo****.*

Big Foot

Irene Plantrich, **Jo's** sister, and her husband, Chuck, have a beautiful home in Northern Michigan. Once, when we were at their home, we made a video I call "Big Foot." **Jo** acted up for the first time that I can remember. I have watched this film over a thousand times; I love to watch it.

When we were at any party, **Jo** would never be in the forefront; she wanted to be at the party and enjoyed it, but desired to be in the background. She enjoyed what was going on, could tell you everything that happened – how many candles on the cake, what the children enjoyed the most – but it was hard to know she was there. **Jo** would sing Happy Birthday, but always in the background.

I can't remember how or who set up this production – it just unfolded out of thin air. Wearing the large, insulated boots hunters wear when they sit in their blinds in the coldest of winters, **Jo** pretended to be Big Foot. Mind you, don't try to walk with these boots on; they are made just to warm your feet while you're sitting.

At the Plantrich home, there is a deck that measures about 30 feet by 20 feet, which can be entered from the corner of the house or out a *doorway from inside the house. I had my video camera at the ready when* ***Jo*** *came around the corner of the house, climbed up two steps, and was on the deck. Making a face as if to scare you, she held out her arms as if to catch you and then laughed her little laugh. Walking in a circle, she said, "I scared away all the deer," and laughed again.* ***Jo*** *had such a nice laugh; if I could only hear it from her now how happy I'd be.*

Jo*, when I first met her, was a 105 pounds of God's creation, but her shoe size was three and a half. She was such a big prize in such a small package. This short footage of video is such a pleasure for me to watch still; I'm so glad I captured her precious performance, which won an academy award in my heart.* ***Jo*** *in any outfit was so attractive. This is the way I will always* **remember my Jo***; look at that smile, so happy.*

We called her "Big Foot" that day
beautiful smile when Jo was at play
She said, "I scared all the deer away"
I told her they weren't meant to stay
The video captured a fun side of Jo
something to cherish I'll never let go
Such joy to watch while we are parted
my flight to heaven will soon be charted
My co-pilot will come to show the way
to be with my Jo, what a glorious day.

SOLAR ORBIT
COORDINATION
EDUCATION
EXERCISE
FUN FOR ALL AGES
TWIRL-A-BALL
SAFE STYROFOAM BALL
CENTRIFUGAL FORCE
REPLACEMENT BALL AVAILABLE
Remember my Jo Ken
MADE IN U.S.A.

35
Years
Later

Solar Orbit

One day, **Jo** and I came up with the idea of making a toy for children. We called it the "Solar Orbit." After attaining a patent, we started our first attempt at a business. I built a jig with the help of my neighbor, Hank; then with **Jo's** help, we built 8,000 Solar Orbits in our garage. Once again wanting it to be a success for **Jo**, I put in many hours pursuing our new project. **Jo**, too, jumped in with her tiny feet and made many phone calls resulting in our first sales order!

You had to see the "Solar Orbit" in motion, so TV was necessary. A lot of money was involved – $58,000 a month for TV commercials alone, which cut deeply into our profits. We have a lot of recordings of the many stores that sold the Solar Orbit – Hudson's, Sears, A&P and many more. It hit several states, as well as the World's Fair in Seattle, Washington.

One afternoon after eight hours work at the missile plant, Hank, who at that time was a small partner in our toy business, rushed out of his house and told me he had just received a call. One of the plants making the Solar Orbit needed more plastic to keep running. He told me he needed help and wanted me to go with him. **Jo** was fixing supper as we rushed in to tell her. She said we should take some time to clean up and then go. "You'll have to eat on the road," she said, "and I don't think you are dressed well enough to be out in public." Hank told her we would be going to a factory to get the plastic, so no one would see us, that it was important to leave now. **Jo** wanted me to take a bath and change into clean clothes. She said she would help and lay out my clothes, but Hank said, "Let's go."

We drove over in his Thunderbird, got the old truck, filled it with gas and headed for Upper Sandusky, Ohio. Hank and his wife, Frieda, drove racecars, and we wasted no time on this trip. It was an impressive factory. Hank told the guard to call the owner of the factory, who soon showed up driving a very handsome, luxury car; he was dressed in an expensive suit and looked the part of a successful business owner. Hank asked him to suggest a good place to eat and he said, "The Country Club." We drove there. It was very impressive, surrounded by more luxury cars, and here we arrive in an old truck.

Hank said, "It'll be okay. Follow me." He had on a bowling jacket with advertisements on the back in big bright letters, but he just barreled ahead. As we entered the dark atmosphere, I hoped that no one would notice us; this was a fancy place and I thought, " we shouldn't be here." The waitress came over and gave us our menus. Hank announced in a very loud voice, "We might not look like it, but we've got money." I shrank under the table. As we were leaving, I saw how nice everyone looked and I felt bad that we had intruded. Once again, **Jo** in her wisdom was so right.

The "Solar Orbit" gave us a year of thrills, meetings, and employment for a lot of people. I counted 30 companies involved, TV, excitement, travel, ups and downs. When it was good, we worked very hard. At one time our partners and lawyers called and said, "When the man I'm talking to signs tomorrow, as he has promised, **Jo** and you will be millionaires!" He was a well-known man who owned a part interest in 100 TV stations. The deal didn't happen, but as always, **Jo** did more than her share. When it went bad ... people not being treated right ... we walked away. **Jo** didn't like anything bad; anything bad and she walked away.

We would often talk about "Solar Orbit" and the good things that came out of it – the nice people we met the people who were employed, the companies involved, and the three million children who got enjoyment out of the toys. We were overjoyed for the experience and excitement; nobody got hurt and we made some money. It gave us a good start in the stock market, too.

Thankfully, we had kept our day jobs! **Jo** and I found out in business who our real friends were. Some who we thought would help didn't, and some we were not sure of came through for us. Sad to say some hoped we wouldn't strike it rich. I'm sure Heaven won't be like that, all good people. **Jo** always rejoiced at anyone's success and she taught me to do the same.

Solar Orbit was a ball in motion
Jo was like that, but she added devotion
She was so helpful with the toy
hoping to give to children some fun and joy
A lot of hard work as we started out
in business you learn what the world's
all about
You have to try and always look forward
in the end you hope your efforts are
rewarded
Each day working with Jo I was blessed
I knew it at the time, as you might
have guessed
It gave a good start to our monetary life
once again, it was because Jo was my
wonderful wife.

3 Chargers

Charger – Our Dog

When Minty, our dog of 8 years, tore a tendon, **Jo** and I both cried when the veterinarian told us that he couldn't save him. We loved him and thanked God for letting us have him. We hated to say good-bye, but there was nothing else to be done. Some months later when we saw a little white Cocker puppy, **Jo** knew this was the one for us. We had two white Dodge Charger automobiles that were the best we could buy, so we choose the name Charger for our beautiful pup. We had him registered as White Charger since the name Charger was already taken. He had the good qualities of all our dogs before him. I wasn't sure why, but this was an exceptional dog from the start. Anyone who cares enough to get a pup should take him to obedience school. When he was at the right age to be trained, we enrolled him.

When we were told only one person could be the handler, **Jo** wanted me to have that honor, but she came to every session and watched from the stands. We talked about his progress on the way home. Charger did us proud and graduated with honors. Some dogs don't make it the first time, you know; they have to be re-enrolled.

Charger was one of our prized possessions and **Jo** took very good care of him; he knew it and showed it by always sticking close by her side. He had such a nice personality. **Jo** and Charger became the best of friends. We took a lot of pictures of the three Chargers; two cars and our remarkable dog, all with the same name. Doglovers were very dazzled with our Charger. If you threw him a ball, he would catch it in his mouth, hang onto it while you threw him a second ball and catch it with his two front paws, hanging on for a long time, while sitting up; he was special. He loved to play ball by himself, too, by dropping the ball from the top of the stairs and running down to the bottom and catching it. He would sometimes wake us up very early in the morning doing that over and over.

At the end of most days, **Jo** and I would set relaxing in our favorite chairs in the family room. Charger would lay down behind an ottoman, his choice place at that time, dog napping and watching us. As we watched T.V., the game for us was to try to get a snack from the kitchen without our loving dog being aware of it. I tried for years, **Jo** joining in once in awhile. If we started to move to get up, Charger would raise his head above the ottoman. When we saw him, we would ease back into our comfortable chairs and he would ease down, too. Whenever he caught us in the kitchen, we shared a snack with him like that had

been our plan all along. We played this game for many years, never being able to open the refrigerator, remove food and get back to our chair without being caught. Then one night **Jo** was triumphant; she even had to call Charger to share her snack. I told you she was an angel. It was the simple things in life and my angel that made me so happy here on earth.

We got a great deal of joy from each dog we had. All our dogs had special qualities and **Jo** brought out their best. We had dogs that I rated as 7 or 8, one was even a 9, but Charger was a solid 10. One day when I let Charger out, he slipped away and did not return when I called and called. When he did not immediately respond, I got a switch and felt when he did get back, he would get a small whipping. I cared a great deal about him and did not want him to get in the habit of wandering away.

I felt I knew the direction he would return, so was watching for him when he came bouncing along so merrily. He spotted me and his joy ended with an abrupt stop. We were about 30 feet apart. I could see his eyes and he saw mine. We began to stare each other down. I slowly went down to one knee to wait him out. He watched me and I watched him for a good minute or two, then suddenly he turned around and looked in the same direction I was looking. I couldn't believe what I was seeing. Did he think I was waiting for some other bad dog?

I laughed and tossed my stick away. I called him to get his attention, and with open arms, grabbed my dog and gave him a hug that brought joy back to both of us. When I told **Jo** what had happened, she laughed with me. It was something we would never forget or ever stop talking to each other about. It was such a special moment. You can see why **Jo** and I felt Charger was the ultimate dog for us.

Jo and Wayne Newton

It was a great year for us. I was working at the Chrysler Missile plant; on the same shift as **Jo**, we were spending all our non-working hours together. The "Solar Orbit," our toy, was launched and doing great. Money was coming in at a fast clip. We purchased a new 1960 Chrysler 300, the fastest car we had ever owned. We had been working so hard; we hadn't had a vacation in a long time. Suddenly we seemed to have things under our control and **Jo** saw the opportunity to take a vacation. She had a long-held desire to see Wayne Newton, but one had to visit Las Vegas to see him perform. A chance to drive the Chrysler 300 in a long road trip excited me, plus making **Jo** happy was within my grasp. I never could think of anything better to do than to spend every minute of the day or night with **Jo**. Since Dad's health was much improved, we could make this trip knowing he would be fine in our absence. **Jo's** mother would take care of our dog and check on the house. **Jo** was so happy; she was bubbling over with joy. Everything would be in harmony when we started for Las Vegas.

When **Jo** told her friends at work of her plans, everyone wanted to help. They knew how hard she worked and how she deserved a great vacation. One business owner told **Jo** to look up his brother, Mr. Francis Compo, who was a pit boss at the Sands Hotel. He said he would call his brother and tell him we were coming, that **Jo** had been so nice to him that he wanted his brother to be extra nice to this remarkable young lady. **Jo** and I had never heard of a pit boss, so we had no idea what help he might be to us.

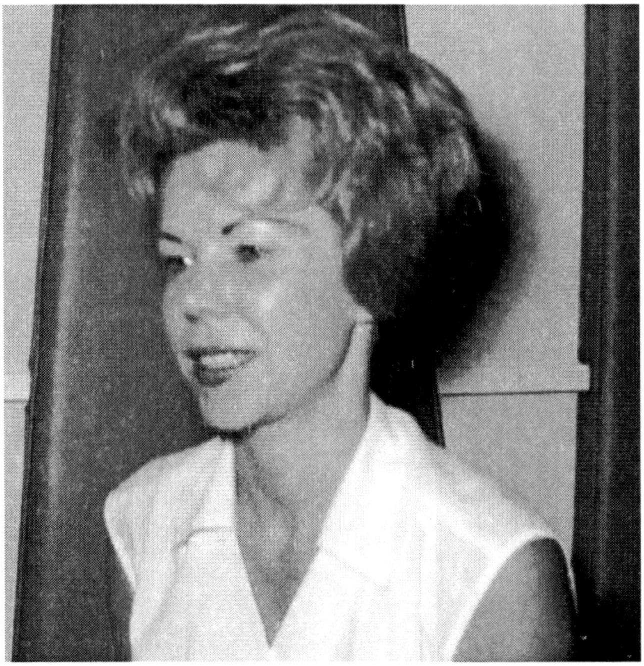

We got out our road maps as most everyone was driving to their destinations in the early 1960's. I knew God was always with my **Jo**, and with God's help, this would be a wonderful trip. It was a clear day when we started. We both had that upbeat feeling now that our trip was finally happening. **Jo** was beautiful, her blue eyes sparkling in anticipation. It showed in everything she did. In the 4,000 miles it would take to drive to Nevada we would see a large part of this spectacular country. It was being with **Jo**, day and night, that would make this trip such a marvelous pleasure for me.

Wherever we went **Jo** always attracted people who were helpful. In Oklahoma we stayed in a motel that had a nice restaurant nearby. There we met a waitress whom, upon seeing our map of Las Vegas, asked if we would like to meet her husband, the chef. She told us he had worked in Las Vegas for several years and had some hints for having a good time there. The first thing he told us was to look for a "sleeper machine." We had no idea what he was talking about. "Some slot

machines pay out more than they take in," he explained. "The small payoffs won't make you rich, but you earn instead of lose. It keeps a lot of bells ringing in the casino. The gambling public only knows that a jackpot has been won. They always think it's the big ones." He told us about some of the best eating places, too, for the best prices and the ones to stay away from. This working couple treated us very nice. **Jo** always wanted to reward kindness, so she reminded me to give them a more-than-generous tip.

The night we arrived in Vegas, the lights dazzled us. Everything was so glamorous – the nightlife, the glitter, the plush carpets, the fancy entrances, the people everywhere dressed in formal wear. We had never seen anything like it. Because she felt she wasn't dressed well enough, **Jo** stayed in the car while I ran into the Sands Hotel. I went to the desk and asked for Mr. Compo only to be told he wasn't on duty that night, but would be in early the next morning. I went back to the car and told **Jo**, then we found a nice place to stay that was very plush and comfortable.

We saw Mr. Compo the next morning. He was about six foot six and weighed well over 300 pounds. He asked us where we were staying. When we mentioned the name of our hotel, he said it was a good place at a fair price. When he asked how much gambling I had done, I told him, "penny ante, nickel-and-dime stuff, small wagers." " Do not play cards here," he warned. "I'll know when to quit," I responded. "We have titles to houses, cars, businesses, yachts, and jewelry," he rejoined, "of people who said that same thing." Looking sternly down at me, he pointed a finger that looked like a club and said, "do what I say. You have a beautiful wife and I don't want to hear you lost big. Play the slots, small coins, but on the strip, not in the big hotels; they will both take your money, but the strip will take it a little slower."

One night when we returned from a show, **Jo** and I noticed a baby-faced boy playing roulette. He was playing all over the board, chips everywhere. He pushed a few chips to the croupier and received lots and lots of chips back for them. The next day I asked Mr. Compo how much this young man was playing for and he went away to find out. When he came back, he said, "he was playing for a quarter million dollars." "That big a game?" I remarked. " That's not much for the real gamblers," Mr. Compo said, "the big games are played in private rooms." I asked, "how can that boy afford to lose so much money?" "When he loses, it's his father's supermarkets. Your money means nothing to them," he said, meaning the owners of the Vegas Casinos. "How hard you work means nothing to them. Be very careful gambling." We met a New York secretary who came to Vegas on a two-week vacation and had been gambling addictively for over 5 years. She worked, but when she got almost enough money to return home to her family, she would just lose it again; gambling can be very bad, indeed.

Mr. Compo helped **Jo** and I with many things in the time we were there. He got us tickets to see Wayne Newton – great seats, the best time for the dinner show, and at a great price. He, also, arranged for **Jo** to get her hair done with the showgirls; **Jo** was mightily impressed. **Jo** looked fantastic dressed so beautifully, and everything around us was so clean and plush. We couldn't have been any happier on that wonderful, marvelous trip. We stopped as we were leaving for home to thank Mr. Compo and tell him we were taking 200 silver dollars home with us. He had a heart to go with his size and was very happy for us.

However, this was not the end of our Vegas trip. When **Jo** got back to work on Monday her boss showed her the phone bill that included several calls to Las Vegas. Mr. Fordan, a very good friend of **Jo's** had called from the office to all the main hotels trying to locate her. He even had the local police looking for our car. If he had found us, we would have been given $20,000 to gamble with. The set-up is that you must spend all the money you were given, but you got to keep all the money you won. When other people see a young couple gambling with big money they say, " why not me?" It's called "being a schill," which means more money for the house in the long run. The Police couldn't find us because we didn't stay in a big name hotel and they couldn't find our car, either, as it had been parked most of the time and we had new plates.

We put the good times, the music, the plush carpets, the clean conditions, and the nice people we met into our memory banks and brought it all back home with us. On our drive back home, some states we traveled through had no speed limits. One day **Jo** was zipping along at 110 mph as we approached a small hill when a gravel truck suddenly appeared in front of us. **Jo** was passing, and he hadn't seen us and turned left in front of her. She swerved into the small ditch and came back on to the road. Her driving had been fantastic. God was surely with us that day. I always felt God was with **Jo** and I was lucky enough to be along for the ride. I had the map out and wrote on it, "**Jo** saved our lives today by her great driving," so you see why I always say, "**Remember my Jo**."

From Monday morning quarterbacking, I found out that Las Vegas was safe because you had only a couple of roads in and out at that time. There was an outstanding police force because the big hotels helped pay for them. Drinks were free while gambling, but I never saw a drunk and there were no fights. There were a lot of churches and very well lit bright areas everywhere. The food was wonderful and the lodgings very reasonable. That all changed in later years, when we returned a few more times to show young people in our family about money. We wanted them to realize you should work for it, rather than gamble your future away.

We returned to Las Vegas for four more trips, but it was never as great as the first time. Each time it had a little more flash, but some of the safeguards were gone. Prices jumped up, also. **Jo** and I were very careful gamblers in the later years and never got hurt in Vegas. While there one year, we received the telegram that the "Solar Orbit" was positioned to make us millionaires.

One of those trips included another opportunity to see Wayne Newton perform. With his beautiful smile and the wholesome show he

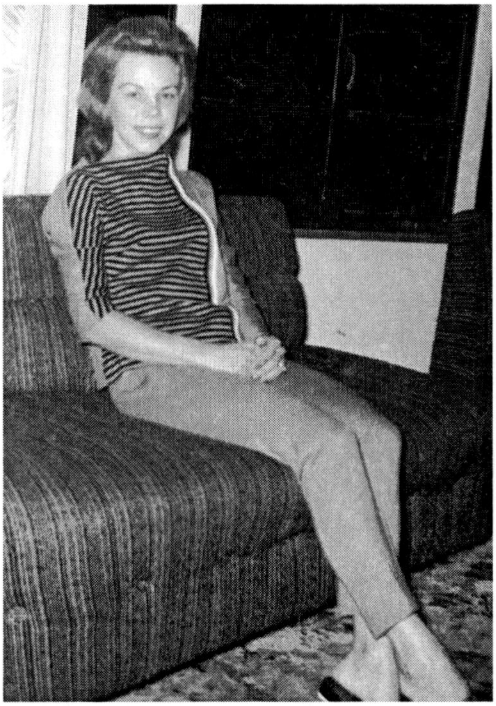

always delivered, it felt like he knew what the audience wanted. He honored this country and always rendered an enthusiastic performance. We had **Jo's** sister Sharon with us. She was living in California and we drove from her home to Las Vegas. On the way back to California, we were able to visit Hoover Dam, which **Jo**, true to her nature, called Hoover Power Plant. Ever proper, **Jo** liked to greet people with "hi," not "hello." I told you she was an angel. Anyway, at the Wayne Newton show, they had some long tables that you would share with others. We sat at our assigned table and three young girls, also from California, joined us. They took to **Jo** from the start, wanting to share their knowledge of Las Vegas with her. They said they would board a bus near Los Angeles, sleep during the drive to Nevada, use hotel coupons for everything, see the shows they wanted, and sleep on the bus again on the return trip home. They told us how to save money on food, lodging, and travel. They even ordered for us so that we would have everything settled before the show started. "Once the show starts no one gets anything," they said, "unless you're in a very high-paying section, which we are not."

Their ultimate goal was to touch Wayne Newton before the night was over. We laughed about that, not believing it possible, but when the lights went down, just as suddenly, they went up again. They announced that the hotel had oversold the show and they were putting a few tables on the edge of the stage. The three young girls bolted at that and secured one of those tables. The show was marvelous, all that we had hoped for. When the house lights went up again, there were the three ecstatic girls at their table on stage. We met them later in the casino and they told us they did, indeed, touch Wayne Newton and had even talked with him. The desire they wanted had come true. My desire is to be with my **Jo**; I trust that this, too, will come true.

To see Wayne Newton was Jo's desire
a fabulous entertainer we always admired
Aristocratic roll model with a beautiful voice
through the year's he was our number
one choice
Seeing Jo and her joy as we arrived
holding her hand, being by her side
Wanting to help Jo, so many reached out
a kindness repayment without a shout
Looking back to gladdening times
always having Jo on my mind.
The marquee's oh, so very bright
for sure my angel belonged in the light.

Age

Chrysler, **Jo's** employer, offered an early retirement to those who could meet the requirements. If they had required the husbands to tell how old their wives seemed to be to them, **Jo** would never have been able to retire in my lifetime. **Jo** was forever young. I've written about her not seeming to age and I think about it constantly, because it was so true. She never seemed over 25 to me. I never felt I was getting older either, because I was with my ageless **Jo**.

Whenever I visualize **Jo**, she is always walking toward me; it all started that warm, summer night at the Conery and lasted a lifetime. The thrill of picking her up always comes to mind. How wonderful it was for all those years. Each week as she left for her beauty appointment, I would tell her how nice she looked. She would always say, "Aw, Ken," and give me a little smile and laugh.

My eyes never wandered. Why would they? Over the years, I heard many sad and pathetic stories about older men and women looking for much younger mates, but I couldn't imagine that for myself when I had **Jo**. My Mother never aged, because she died so young, but I don't think she would have aged for my Father ever. It's what's called true love.

You can't remember something that didn't happen and it can't be called history unless it happened. Some people enter educational institutions to devote their lives to history. I've devoted my life to the history of my **Jo**; it is what this book is about. I have the joy of reliving the history of my life with **Jo**. It gives me such joy to recall my happy and wonderful life; I relive it every day in my mind. I pick out a couple of stories that I have written to reminisce about, then I play a recording of her voice, look at some of the pictures, watch the videos, read a few *of her letters, and let my mind travel back in time. I look forward to remembering my* **Jo** *every day of the rest of my life here on earth.*

Remember my Jo is what I do
her smile, her laugh, her eyes so blue
She could make each day begin
without her nothing's left for Ken
Because we parted
so broken-hearted
Until we are together for me all is lost
I'll honor my Jo forever at any cost.
Forever young
Jo will always be
She will never grow old
Or age for me
Building on the past
True love will always last
God guaranteed
That love last eternally.

Inventions

With the success of the Solar Orbit and all the hours of talk about inventions, Dad decided he wanted to work with me to invent something beneficial to all. Dad had the hardest and best teeth his dentist had ever seen. Dr. Hladan told us Dad's teeth would burn up the best drills he had, even if it was just a little cavity. Dad wanted to help other people have better dental hygiene with this new invention of his – the water-powered toothbrush. When I told **Jo** that we would work together, she said, "count me in, too. I think it's wonderful."

Dad had the machinery to start the project and, in a short time, we had a model of what we wanted. It was such a pleasure to work with Dad; he was so knowledgeable and proficient in anything he did. We contacted the Fuller Brush Company and found we could use a brush on our invention that they had for another item. We filed a patent immediately; it was 1961 and there were no other power-toothbrushes on the market. Dad, **Jo**, and I were very optimistic about its profit potential.

A local industrialist, Jim Robbins, had built a new plastic plant that was quite successful. Once a year he would finance one new product, so Dad and I went to his office to show our invention to the proper people. We were sitting in the waiting room when some ducks walking through surprised us. The staff told us that they opened a front and back door at the same time each day for these ducks to cross through to their marshland habitat. We hoped they would be as considerate with our toothbrush idea as they were with the ducks. Sad to say, it didn't happen that way; we came in second.

We put all our hopes on submitting again the next year as Mr. Robbins people had suggested, but a few months later Broxident, a *large corporation, came out with a battery-operated device that would have put us out of business. Dad and I agreed to walk away from the idea, glad we hadn't lost our financial shirts. We had had a great time working together, we didn't get hurt financially, and the three of us had enjoyed the adventure.*

Dad kept trying to invent other things throughout` the years, because he enjoyed the challenge and it kept him feeling and thinking young. Like Dad, I would think up inventions in my spare time. Some years ago, I came up with an idea for an energy device that would replace most present day energy sources. Its cost is low, its pollution output is almost nil, and it would end the United State's dependency on foreign oil, plus it would increase employment in every state. With the United States marketing this device, we would be the envy of every nation. I don't believe the supply of this power device would ever meet the demand in our lifetime.

I have passed this idea on to the next generation and, with God's help, it will someday be produced. There would be a small device installed in each home and a larger device for companies and public utilities. There would be no more power failures, weather would never be a factor, and there would be no pollution. When you start to use the Roberts-Plantrich-Murphy water generator, remember that you read about it first right here. Help make this a better world by remembering my ***Jo****, as she helped immeasurably with this project.*

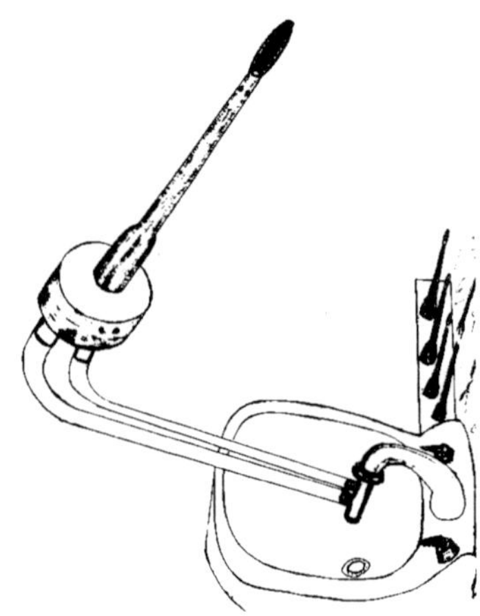

Etiquette

Jo was always kind. How seldom I see that today. She always thanked me any time I opened a door, passed the salt, or helped her on with her coat. If I said, "you don't have to thank me," she would always say, " I want to, Ken." She always wanted me to understand that she appreciated what I did for her. I would do anything I could for her, because she had done so much for me. We never took each other for granted.

Jo always returned telephone calls, never leaving anything undone. She answered the phone thoughtfully, and if it was a wrong number, she tried to help the person. She would even call to apologize for someone else, asking if there was anything she could do to correct the wrong that had been done. What a joy it was to be around **Jo**.

I miss **Jo** and her kindness so much. That, "Aw, Ken," with her little laugh was kindness at its best. I hope other people will think of the benevolence that **Jo** tried to spread around and keep it going. If the attention to detail and gentle assistance that **Jo** gave to this world spread, it would mean no more fighting. Compassion can eradicate wars.

Mother and **Jo** were always reading a book about etiquette, so they could help make the world a better place. Their being in Heaven now with my Dad makes me feel that I need to be with them to complete my journey.

Selective

I was working afternoons and **Jo** was on days as always, when I took my car to the Dodge dealer for routine maintenance. I liked to stroll the showroom whenever I was there. A salesman friend of ours rushed over to me when he saw me admiring the new cars, telling me he had a very special car that **Jo** was sure to like. I went with him to see it and was very impressed. It was special and I thought **Jo** would certainly like it. Don Buslep, the salesman, asked if he could show it to **Jo** that night, adding, "this car will sell real quick and I think **Jo** should have it."

I called **Jo** at work and told her that Don would be bringing this beautiful car by and I said, " if you want it, it's yours." That evening **Jo** was waiting for Don, hoping she would see a car she would want. He took her for a ride and asked her what she thought. "It's a wonderful-looking car, but it's not for me," she said. " What's wrong with it?" he asked. " I don't think anything is wrong with it," she said, " it's just not for me." Don called me the next day and told me 99 out of 100 women would have grabbed that car. "**Jo** is 1 in more than a million," I said, "you'll sell us more cars, Don, just not this one."

If **Jo** liked something, she would let you know and it would get the best of care. She didn't buy for the joy of buying. I didn't understand this at first, but living with and loving **Jo**, I learned how wonderful her outlook on life was. She was not spoiled, but rather she was loving and caring. She, over the course of her lifetime, saved us lots of money, because she wouldn't buy something she didn't want.

Even though **Jo** did not want this car, she and Don remained good friends. We purchased several more new cars from him, too. He learned that **Jo** was one in more than a million, a fact I had known from our first meeting. If you are lucky enough to find someone like **Jo**, enjoy your life together like I did.

Ohio

Whenever, Dad's wealthy Uncle Al Roberts visited Ohio, he had a doctor and nurse attending him day and night. His lungs were the problem. He spent 95 % of his time in Albuquerque, New Mexico, because his doctors recommended the hot, dry climate. He was a prosperous man and could afford anything that could make him feel more comfortable. As his health failed, Uncle Al spent less time each year away from Albuquerque. His fortune was growing, but his life was slipping away. He couldn't improve his health, but he was courageous, brilliant, religious, and a help to others. Dad spent hours talking with him, but all we kids got was a pat on the head and a coin from his pocket. Dad would talk to us about him on our drive home from Ohio, commenting on how sad his life was becoming because of his distressed health.

Ferral Roberts, Uncle Al's daughter, was married to Berch Laymon, a very remarkable man. They had four children that Uncle Al always wanted to see, if he was able. He traveled in the largest trailer I had ever seen up to that time. It was equipped with innumerable things he might need. We visited him at his home, too, that was the best money could build, located in New Vienna, Ohio, the town that he owned – the bank, all the stores, the waterworks, the *power company, the movie house – you name it, he owned it. He owned several farms and gainfully employed a lot of people. He supplied the school bus system with fine transportation in a very large area. Uncle Al had a temporary outdoor movie house built, so he could see movies from his bedroom. It was the first drive-in-movie I had ever seen. The whole community saw the movies at no charge. We watched it from his front porch. When I went shopping with his grandchildren in New Vienna, anything they wanted in the stores was put on grandpa's tab and paid for later.*

The Fourth of July fireworks was at a golf course just outside of town. There were rockets tied to the surrounding fence posts. People came in hay-wagons to see this huge display. Berch was a fine man and a capable farmer, but with the control of the farm still in his father-in-law's hand he always felt slighted. Uncle Al was only protecting his wife's interests, because he knew his time was very limited on this earth, but it made for some hard feelings. Still no one really suffered from what we could see. They were all very well provided for. During his life, Uncle Al had purchased several rental homes, putting the rent into bank accounts for the grandchildren. They would all be rich at a very young age.

Berch lost his arm in a thrashing machine accident when he was about 40. He told Dad and I privately that when he took off his artificial arm before retiring at night, he didn't feel like a whole man. We both told him that that was not so, assuring him that he was a real man's man. Their 200-acre farm was not large enough in later years, so they began to raise cattle and show animals. They had automatic feeders, a system to clean out the barn, and lots of concrete walks and runways. They also rented out large machinery to other farmers. The last couple of times we saw Berch and Ferral they had a little dog with them. They told us they didn't like air conditioning in cars, but they got it so they could leave the little dog in the car in hot weather. The dog liked it!

After Dad retired he bought 10 acres of land in Ohio that used to be the local church's picnic ground. There he built his last house. One day Dad was visiting a farmer friend who said he had a young chick that was being pecked by all the other chickens. "They sometimes will kill a new chick," he said, asking Dad if he would take it to his farm. Dad said he would try to save it. Having no chickens, he put it in with his three ducks, thinking the ducks wouldn't hurt this little chick. In a very short time the ducks and the chick were the best of friends. It was very obvious that this chick thought he was a duck, because he waddled as he walked; however, he would not enter any water like the ducks would. I believe this shows that you learn a great deal from the family you grow up with. Some things are genetic, but not everything.

I told **Jo** about my wealthy relatives and she got to meet them in later years. **Jo** and I got to see Ferral and Berch a lot when we would visit Dad, because their properties were near one another. They all loved **Jo** and she could feel the love they had for her. Berch took to **Jo** very quickly. The Laymon family always had plans for us whenever they knew we were coming.

The youngest Laymon son, Albert, was on his way to church one Sunday morning when he was killed in a freak truck accident. We attended the funeral at the Laymon home. It was very sad. We couldn't understand then or now, why this happened. It's so hard to comprehend the human tragedies that happen here on earth. I can't understand why **Jo** had to leave me so soon, either. God only knows, and one day, so will I. "I'll love you for ever and ever, amen," one of the lyrics from one of our favorite songs keeps running through my mind.

Exposure

It seems like only yesterday, but many years ago I came home and told **Jo** this story. I knew she'd enjoy it, because her personal philosophy was that you should look your very best while always being polite and friendly.

I had stopped at a local McDonald's restaurant to get a snack to take home. It was near lunchtime and the line of cars waiting at the drive-thru window was very long. I thought the line would move faster inside, so I parked my car and went in. While I was standing in line, I noticed a very well dressed gentleman standing in the line across from me. I know expensive suits when I see them and this, believe you me, was a very expensive suit.

We both reached the order counter about the same time. Placing our orders side-by-side I heard every word he said. After placing his order, he asked if he could talk to "that nice-looking young fellow for a minute." When the boy he had indicated approached, he asked, " do you like horses, young man?" "I do, sir," the young man cheerfully answered. "Here is my card," he said, "I have a stable of very fine horses and would like to talk with you someday soon about your future. I look forward to hearing from you." The boy thanked him and stepped back, quickly glancing at the card as the man received his order and left with a wave of his hand. All the young boys and girls rushed to see the card the man had given to their friend. They began asking him rapid-fire questions, becoming a celebrity in an instant. He looked so happy hanging onto that card that held his future. I noticed how small, neat and trim he was. He would, indeed, make a fine jockey. As I was leaving the restaurant, I saw the man in the expensive suit drive away in an equally expensive automobile.

*I told **Jo** what I had witnessed and what a great future this young boy might have. **Jo** said, "if he was neat, clean and polite, I know he will have a great future." We both pondered this chance meeting of two human beings, thinking about how the young boy's having been exposed in such a good light opened the door to an opportunity that could change his life forever. I felt sure that when that boy left home that morning he had no idea of what was about to happen to him, but that he always naturally looked his best at whatever he did, proving **Jo's** personal philosophy right again.*

Jo Cooked with Love

Jo loved life. She was always wanting to please herself and others, as well as stay healthy. She wanted to enjoy the pleasures of food without doing harm to what God had created. She cooked with love and hoped she was doing the best for anyone who sat at our table. What more could you ask of Angel **Jo**? We ate fruit and vegetables moderately and we had meat four or five times a week. Dad was diabetic and **Jo** cooked for him for many years, meticulously weighing the food and counting the calories. He loved her for the care she would take.

Jo always honored her mother and she grew up cooking in order to make it easier on her working mother. It was always her desire to please the people she loved without them knowing that it was planned. **Jo** made a meat loaf for me that would melt in my mouth and my appetite would demand more and more. She understood that I liked a lot of foods that didn't like me and would make special dishes for her and me. I liked sauerkraut, but my body said, "no way." **Jo** found out that if she burnt it, I loved it and so did my body. I thanked her because it was so good and because she had found the answer for me. She learned to like things I liked. I never heard her complain, and she always smiled when I told her of the enjoyment I got from her kindness. My Angel always had the answer to every problem.

I told her how I loved the special cooking she did for me. Most of our lives we ate to stay alive, but when **Jo** cooked her special dishes made with love; we lived to eat more and more. I could eat her pumpkin bread forever. She could make bean soup so special that we always ate too much, but still looked forward to eating even more.

Jo's cooking was very special every Easter, Thanksgiving and Christmas. She always fixed turkey and ham with all the trimmings. I would always assist her, but the credit and final outcome was because of her desire to please the people she had invited to her table. We continuously checked the roaster and each dish she was preparing. She put love in everything she did, remember she was my Angel. At Christmas, **Jo** made dozens and dozens of cookies which took one, sometimes two, full days of work. They made a lot of people all over the country happy during the holiday season. Her recipes went with her to heaven and the loving touch she had is gone from earth.

Food, day after day, can become dull at times and, I guess it has to be that way. **Jo**, day after day, was never monotonous. When it came to special cooking for me, **Jo** was always remarkable. My love for **Jo** would extend for eternity. That's the one thing I am sure of. I hope you find an Angel for you; if you haven't yet, keep looking. I found mine and soon will be with her again. I envision **Jo** with my Mother and Dad having such a good time together. God wants love and happiness all around him. It was why we were put on this earth, to find the right people to love, and be with, in Heaven. When I am again with the astounding people I write about, my love will join theirs in an eternal circle.

Jo was beauty in motion

No matter what I was doing, **Jo** would calmly flit into the picture, without announcing that she was assisting. What a joy it was to have her appear. Every job I decided to do, I was sure she would help me. If I started to wash the car and she was in the house cleaning, like a lovely butterfly soon she's there washing windows inside the car. I rush around doing the wheels and when I move around, the next wheel has already been done looking better than the ones I've finished. I backtrack to make those I've already done look as good as **Jo's**. She had so much love inside her it spilled over, making everything shiney and new.

The letter carrier passed and I got the mail and took it in the house to post. When I returned, she had nearly finished the car. "Put the car in the garage and come in for lunch," she said. The lunch is there on the table all ready and has her individual touch; **Jo** was up to her old tricks.

When she's working behind the tool shed at the back of our property, I would sometimes say, "nobody will see what you have done," and she would say, "I will." What wonderment she was. She felt that any possession of hers would be taken care of to the best of her ability. She was so proud of everything she possessed or was near and I was always so proud of her. Most people can only do what they can do; I saw **Jo** do much more, because she was an angel.

At the end of each day, we could retire to bed knowing a dignified amount of progress had been made and the world was a better place for it. "Cleanliness is next to Godliness," **Jo** would say, living that way all her life. **Jo** thanked God every night for the life we were living and honored those we had known. She was beauty in motion at all times.

She was interested in anything I started and always ready to assist me without saying a word. It's the love she had and her desire to help all those she loved. I knew that any project I started, flit, **Jo** would be there. It made me aware of my progress. I think she is helping me now with the writing of this book. "Thank you, **Jo**," I whisper, "I love you and always will."

With Jo around things would improve
She desired to help with a positive move
She seldom announced or wanted recognition
Jo would flit in and out, not needing permission
It was her desire to help all she could
Those knowing Jo always understood
Flitting in and out, not being seen
working like a well-oiled machine
If it was done to perfection and I had to know
I'd look around and for sure would find Jo.

Tornado

I had been working Downriver at the Marathon Oil refinery for just a short time when **Jo** and I had our new home built in West Bloomfield. I took pictures into work one day of the progress we were making to show my fellow employees; I was so proud of what **Jo** and I were doing. The oil refinery was 15 miles from our home, so no one from work had been out in our area; they only knew the house from my pictures and what I'd told them about it.

A couple of years later when I was talking about my beautiful **Jo** and our attractive home, one of the guys said, "When are we going to see **Jo** and that home you're so proud of?" That night I asked **Jo** if we could have the guys I worked with and their wives out for a party and she said, "why not!" We had had friends and relatives over several times and things had always worked out great. We decided to invite ten couples and together we carried it out. **Jo** put everything in motion; we catered food, got in drinks, and set it all up for a Saturday night. Our home was set in the woods and it got very dark at night. We were on a dirt road in an undeveloped area, so I passed out maps at work. I was asked how they could find my house and I jokingly told them, "it's the house with no lights on and nobody home," which got a good laugh.

On the appointed Saturday night, just a few minutes before their arrival time, West Bloomfield had a complete power failure. That's right, no lights! **Jo** rushed around to find candles to light, as I went to find some flashlights. Never having had a power failure in this house before, it was very hard for **Jo** and I to move around in total darkness, but we had to do something. In a few minutes, we were going to have 20 people in our house, the wives all total strangers to **Jo** and I. We couldn't take them in the dark downstairs to our recreation room. Step down floors, Oh no! The bathrooms weren't working, we couldn't

make coffee, and even the doorbell wouldn't chime. It was raining heavily and the wind had picked up, when we saw the first car lights outside. I went out with a flashlight and started leading the couples in. What a night for a party!

The guys and their wives were taking in all in stride and busily making lots of suggestions, but there was no real solution to our power outage problem. Just then the phone rang; it was **Jo's** mother, calling to ask if we were all right saying, "The news reported a tornado in West Bloomfield." **Jo** told her we were without power, but had no other problems – other than a house full of strangers sitting in the dark! **Jo** relayed the information that a tornado had hit about four miles from us. The power was restored in about 30 minutes, but everyone had enjoyed sitting in the soft candlelight talking and laughing about the situation with one another. Our guests stayed four more hours. It took some time for things to get fully back to some kind of order. As they filed out the door at the end of the evening, everyone said they liked the house and had enjoyed themselves. **Jo** was her beautiful self as always and had saved the day with her calmness in the face of the storm.

As I expected when I went into work on Monday, one of the guys who'd been to our house said, "don't go out to the Roberts home, they have tornadoes." I retorted, " you guys caused the tornado, racing your cars on the expressways going out there; next time drive a little slower." We all laughed. Throughout the 24 years I worked at Marathon, we had a lot of those same people out for other parties. We worked hard and built strong friendships, as well as a beautiful house. My best friends told others at work about my beautiful **Jo** and how gracious she was. Everyone that met **Jo** enjoyed her friendship.

The guests arrived
a speedy drive
That storm was near
I had no fear
My wife and I continued our
show
even a tornado couldn't stop
my Jo

Recreation Room

Passing our home from the street, one would think, " nice house." Entering one would say, "different." Spending some time here you would say, "**unique**." One of the most unique rooms in our home is the recreation room, which **Jo** was involved in from start to finish.

The first thing you see as you walk down a white plush carpeted stairway would be a sign that reads, "**Jo**-Ken, Bar, Casino & Recreation." On the ledge along that stairway would be models of cars we once owned. The landing at the bottom of those steps is carpeted. On the wall to the left is an optical illusion painting of a hallway exit. **Unique**.

Along the north wall is a wooden phone booth, then New York, New York, Frank Sinatra City. Sinatra was **Jo's** favorite singer of all time. I sketched the city scene that was behind Sinatra when he was performing. A local artist was to transfer my small drawing onto the 27-foot wall, but when she didn't **Jo** and I did the best we could. We were always satisfied with, and even proud of, what we had done. **Unique**.

A real stoplight is at the corner of the 33-foot east wall. Then there is an accumulation of beer signs, a fire alarm that at one time was in a school, a Juke box, a Pepsi machine, a Vernor's barrel with a Flint mobile on top of it, a coin-operated weigh machine, a Popcorn wagon, a Player piano, and at the corner a "walk safety" walklight. Unique, again.

The south wall has a hat rack where some of **Jo's** hat collection is hung, then there is a 6-foot doorway leading outside to a staircase that leads to the spa room. Next to that is a Pachinco machine, a "Berserk" video game, a Pinball machine, a Vegas slot machine and a corner table of games viewed on a color Television. Unique.

The Cheers bar was **Jo's** idea. When she first suggested it, I jokingly said it could not be done, but it wasn't too long before we had designed the layout, got in touch with our builder, and were off and running. With its 10 high-back stools and tigerlily decor, it is fully equipped for large or small parties.

The 30-foot west wall has 2 sets of swinging saloon doors that frame a booth specifically built to match the tigerlily orange leather decor of the "Cheers" bar. Over 30 people can sit on stools, chairs, and the booth in this unique recreation room.

Jo wanted clean, neat, comfortable, and gratifying surroundings. She made this a place where one could have music, bright decor, and fun-filled times. We had lots of parties that everyone, young and old alike,

enjoyed. Add a pool table, disco lights, a hand chair, exercise bike, punching bag, special lighting and card table and anyone visiting was more than entertained from the moment they entered the recreation room. This was a place to eat, sing, dance, play games, read books, look at albums, hear wonderful music and have games for all ages.

Jo was very satisfied with what we had put together. It was a lot of hard work, searching and tracking down the people necessary to put it all together. It was good, clean fun and ended up being rewarding to us. The memories of the good times we spent in this room are immeasurable. **Jo** was so delightful in nice surroundings, with soft music playing. Anything **Jo** was around would sparkle. If she put on the Hope diamond, its magnificence would increase. Her blue eyes would make it glitter more.

Spa Room

Jo saw a picture in a magazine of a movie star's spa room that she liked. Showing it to me, I agreed it was for us. She called Lino Biolichini, the contractor who built our house. Lino, his wife, and daughter had been our neighbors at one time. He had a couple of houses, big ones, being built by him and his crews, so he was busy, but he had always liked **Jo** and agreed to get help to do this work.

I drew what I thought was the plan that would fit our house; **Jo** looked it over and we began another project. First, I had to break out the old patio; Lino had put reinforced wire in the slab, so it meant a lot of hard work. It had been the right way to build it, and the spa room would also be built Lino's way, the right way. Lino gave us a lot of help. We used his truck and he went with me to order the materials. **Jo** was making phone calls, doing her fair share.

*Lino ordered the glass: two doorwalls and 14 panels of special-cut glass for the skylight. This was to be a big job using special equipment – picking out the spa, special sand, power unit, heater, large beams, lights, and accessories. We picked out the flooring at the stone yard, every piece. Lino and **Jo** and I put the floor in, with each piece fitting closely against the others. **Jo** wanted to include a stairway to the recreation room which was a great idea. The spa room with track lighting turned out to be beautiful, one-of-a-kind. It was a **Jo** original*

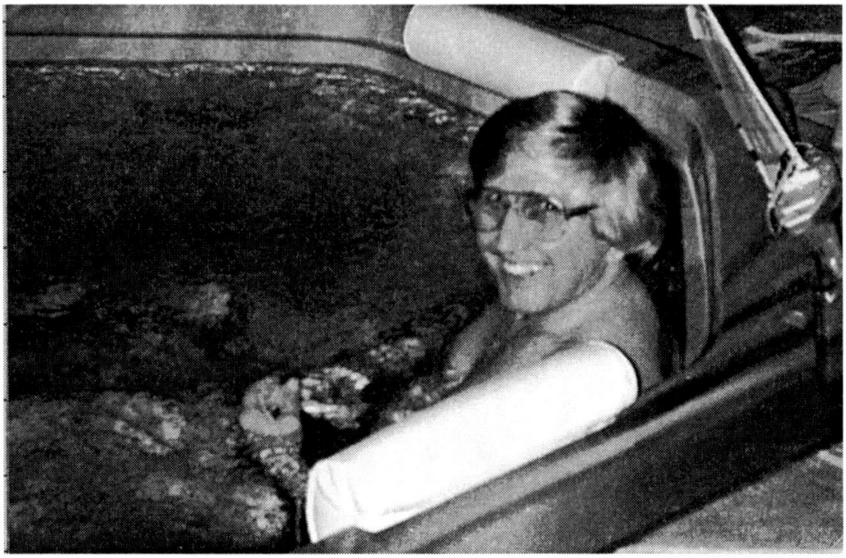

– that is why I loved her more each day. She and I finished something clean, elegant, and fun for everyone who used it.

I cherished the time I had with **Jo**; she was so precious to me. In this life you need a loved one to share your hopes and dreams with. I don't have that anymore. I won't start any more projects or draw any more plans; my heart wouldn't be in it. As always, I need my **Jo** to spark me. I need her to derive joy from anything I do.

Mailbox

Lino Biolichini's construction crew had finished our spa room and there was a considerable amount of quality lumber left over. I asked ***Jo****, who always provided the spark for any of my home improvement projects, "what should I build with the beautiful lumber?" "Build us a special mailbox, Ken," she said, "and I want to help you." "Great idea,* ***Jo****," I replied, "it'll be the first thing you see as you near our home." I knew we could do it. We were both retired and enjoying life with one another to the fullest.*

I selected the pieces of wood I would need, and since it was cold outside, I moved into the basement to build the mailbox ***Jo*** *and I had designed. It would be a low maintenance A-Frame; strong and sturdy, but not too large. It would be a neat, clean, attractive mailbox that was worthy of being in our neighborhood; a mailbox that would make* ***Jo*** *and I proud to say we made it ourselves. We would use the same stain as the interior and exterior of our spa room which we had stained ourselves. With* ***Jo's*** *help and love, this mailbox would be a snap. I* told her, "I'll do the best I can," and she said, "Aw, Ken, I know you will, it'll be beautiful." The mailbox project was a labor of love, because it would please my **Jo**.

I started on the mailbox and **Jo** was in and out several times, keeping everything orderly and clean. She was doing her usual household routine, but would take time to compliment the progress I was making. I've told you how I usually rushed around and how she slowed me down, forcing me to take a break, with snacks and her special "slow down" method. **Jo**, in her discrete way, kept me from making mistakes.

She took pictures of the beautiful finished product to prove our love for this joint venture. Talking about mail now that **Jo** is no longer here, I remember that **Jo's** love was always delivered. During the war I could always count on **Jo** for joy at mail call. "Please, God, if I can't get a phone call from my beloved wife," I now pray daily, "then forward a letter to me from my **Jo**; I know my angel would write, if you promised to send it. It would help greatly, until I am with her again. You know how I love and miss her."

Pepsi

I looked in the Sunday paper and ran across a Pepsi machine for sale, about 20 miles from our home. Three young fellows had been running an auto repair shop and used the Pepsi machine to keep beer and pop cold. They were going out of business and wanted to sell the items that they could. I asked **Jo** if she would like to go for a ride and take a look at it? She went with me. We drove up to a nice house and were informed that the machine was in the garage in the back. It had started to snow, so we made a dash for the garage. **Jo** and I looked at the pop cooler; we felt it would be a great asset to our recreation room. It needed paint and some trays repaired, a good cleaning and a little TLC. **Jo** would give it all the TLC it needed.

It weighed a lot, so it would have to be delivered. Agreeing on a price including delivery, they promised to deliver before dark the next day. It was winter, so it got dark early. Expecting them by 6 p.m., **Jo** and I rushed home from work. At 10 p.m., they called asking if they could still deliver it; **Jo** said, "since you're nearby, come ahead."

It was dark, a foot of snow on the ground, not ideal conditions to make the delivery. It was still snowing when a wreck of a truck rolled down our road backfiring, steaming and almost out of control. The three young men piled out of the truck like it was a summer day. They were late because the truck had broken down; auto repairmen, my foot.

The machine would have to be brought in the Recreation room doorway. I showed one of the men the path they would have to bring the machine through a foot of freshly-fallen snow. The answer was, "no problem, we have a dolly and plywood," but the dolly couldn't be used because it had only one handle and the plywood broke the second they tried to put it to use. My first impression was that they were a sad bunch

of fellows who did not prepare for the job, however, after spending more than five hours with these young men in our Recreation room, I discovered they were well- mannered gentlemen. **Jo** talked to each one and felt the same as I did – in the right jobs they might have a great future.

They tried all the games and we all were having a great time together. They played the player piano, juke box, pinball, and slot machines, played pool, and had fresh popcorn; when I looked at my watch it was 3 a.m.! I said; "**Jo** and I have to go to work today." "That's okay, Mr. Roberts," they said, "we'll take care of everything for you." They left thirty minutes later. **Jo** and I jumped into bed, got a couple hours sleep, took our showers and went to work. Once again **Jo** had put somebody else's concerns, the young men's desire to deliver the Pepsi machine, ahead of her wishes. She told me they had come so far that we should think of them. We retired the next night very early, needless to say.

In a few days we had the Pepsi machine working, looking like new. We filled it with pop, put all the trays in, tested it, and again **Jo** had done more than her share. Those tiny feet made every step of this project a pleasure. Nice people, nice project, good transaction for all. Some plans get stretched out; my plan to be with **Jo** is being stretched out now. I want to be with my **Jo** again.

Juke Box

The words juke box means "coin-operated phonograph." Neither **Jo** nor I knew that. We, also, didn't know it was a protected business, of "Big Men," if you know what I mean. They were not for sale to the public.

A couple of days after Christmas **Jo** said, "I didn't get what I wanted for Christmas." "What was that?" I asked. "I wanted a juke box." "You didn't mention a juke box, I hadn't heard the word before," I said. "I didn't know until Christmas day that we were having a New Year's Eve party," **Jo** said, "and I would like to have a juke box by then." "It would be impossible to even rent a machine by party time," I said. "Here is the phone book; find me someone to talk to." She was on the phone about five minutes when she handed me the receiver and told me to take down some instructions. The man on the phone asked

Jo's Mom

me where I worked and what time I got off. He then said, "go to this abandoned gas station, pull in at 7:00 p.m., four men will be in a Ford station wagon, we'll blink our lights and you follow." When I hung the phone up, ***Jo*** *said, "You're not going to do that, are you?" "Sure," I said," I won't have the money on me and you want a juke box, don't you?" "Yes," she softly said.*

The next day after work, I drove to the abandoned gas station and pulled in. Lights blinked from the wagon, I followed. We drove in and out of side streets, so that I couldn't find this place in the daylight without solid instructions. In the middle of a large city block, we drove into a large parking lot, office up front, warehouse in the back – a big warehouse!

Four burly men got out of the station wagon. One said, "Follow me." We walked into the big warehouse that was filled with a lot of damaged jukeboxes and pinball machines. Broken legs, glass missing, some sort of vending machines I hadn't ever seen before. They must have come from bars that had had terrible fights in them, things I knew nothing about. The man asked me to pick out one from a special area; they weren't in too bad shape. When I picked one, he said, "No, that one is hard to get parts for if you have trouble with the sound." I picked another and he said, "I'll have that ready when you come back tomorrow. You can pick out 60 new records," he said, as he handed me some printed sheets to show ***Jo****, so she could pick out some of the records she might like.*

I returned the following day with the money. The same big guy plugged in the jukebox, played a couple of records. Then he took me to a door at the end of the warehouse. He pushed a buzzer and said "go down the long hallway and turn right to the record section." I had gone about 50 feet when another big man stepped out of an office, picked me up by my clothes and asked how I got in. I told him "Frank let me in." He took me back to the warehouse, confirmed my story with Frank, and then let me proceed on. It was a nice record section, but it was hard to find the records **Jo** and I wanted. You had to know your way around, which I didn't. I, nevertheless, got the new records and Frank got me a lot of used ones. Frank and another man followed me home in that station wagon. They set the jukebox up and got it playing. They met **Jo**; Frank said how delightful she was. He told me to get in touch with him about a pinball machine if I wanted one, which I did later in the year. They made us promise not to sell the machines unless we sold them back to them.

I never asked **Jo** what she had said to Frank on the phone that night, but I am sure it was her voice and how she said what was necessary to get us the jukebox. We did have trouble with the pinball machine and Frank sent out someone to fix it at no charge. Both the jukebox and the pinball machine are still working fine. We always have money for you to play and we keep the drawer open, so the money comes back. It's a break-even situation and a lot of fun to play the professional machines.

I remember that New Year's Eve party, the first one with the jukebox. It was **Jo's** doing. She could do so much in such a short time. I did not believe it possible at the time and I still find it inconceivable that this came off like clockwork. **Jo** could do the unattainable with ease

Picture of Jo's mom

Player Piano

Ernie, a friend of mine from work, was helping me paint the trim on my house. We were taking breaks in our recreation room. When he asked, "With all the things you have, why no player piano?" I said, "We would like one, but haven't gotten around to it." "You got one now," he said. When Ernie moved into his house, the piano was in the basement; his daughters had played it until it wouldn't play anymore. He said the rolls were no good anymore and he was going to junk it if I didn't take it. He joked that it would make good firewood.

Coming home from work one day, I stopped by his house and took a look at it; it was in sad shape, but had a good sounding board. That's the most important part to old pianos. I arranged for a piano moving company to take it to my home. Moving the piano from Ernie's house required removing some of the trim off his basement door. Being a carpenter, Ernie did the work himself; he wouldn't take any money, said "no charge" because of **Jo**.

It was a 1902 Stuyvesent Pianola, Aeolian Company, with metrostyle themodist, the finest player of its time made in New York. We soon found out that a lot of hard work was needed to save this player piano. The outer finish was blistered; the bellows and tubing had deteriorated. **Jo** was more than willing to give it a try and was soon on the phone lining up what was needed. **Jo** and I did the outer stripping of the blistered sections in 3-hour sessions every night for about a month. The wood turned out to be beautiful because of **Jo** and the hard work she insisted on doing. We bought the best oil we could to give it the proper treatment. A lot of hard work and $2000 later, we had a gem of a machine and a great story to go with it.

It was a project that **Jo** took great interest in, she wanted it done right. I always needed her help, because I tend to rush into things. I mean well, but haste doesn't turn out the best results. **Jo** lined up two men who would fix, repair and replace what was needed to preserve this phenomenal piece of history.

One of the men came and took out the inside bellows; tubing, key hammers and platforms needed to reconstruct the inner works. It was a much bigger job than most people could imagine. If you think of it, the player piano takes some holes on paper and produces remarkable music to sing and dance to. By pumping two pedals you can have a marvelous, enjoyable night or day of entertainment. Even a child or person of any age can feel wonderful; the joy this produces and the day and time it was invented is unbelievable.

Mark Haas, a blind gentleman whose job it is to restore and tune pianos was one of the men **Jo** hired. She spent a lot of time with Mr. Haas and was very impressed with his accomplishments. Mr. Haas tuned, made some final adjustments and, in no time, because of the improvement in bellows, tubing and the material used, it was playing better than new. Haas, and the other man, were very satisfied with the music it put out. Haas also put in a motor you could pump or have it play by itself.

I visited the shop where some of the work was being performed; it took a lot of planning to reconstruct the tubing, bellows and platforms that all this had to be set up for. Then a lot of work had to be done in our recreation room. We still have the picture and an article about Mr. Haas that ran in the regional newspaper. We recommended him to some other people who hired him; they were as impressed as we had been. He was a wonderful, astonishing man and **Jo** and I felt blessed for knowing him and sharing this experience.

I thought I would have to search for player piano rolls, but **Jo** found a toll free number of a company that would deliver the rolls to your front door – Elvis or any other musician you had ever heard of. **Jo** and I got the catalogs and ordered what we wanted. Long-playing, beautiful, up-to- date music. Long-playing at the click of a switch. Why does a player piano sound so good? It's because of the number of fingers that are on the keys. An artist can even accompany himself by playing a second time.

I forwarded the information on our 1902 Stuyvesent Pianola to an historical group and they told us we had a priceless piece of equipment made by the old masters. This was possible all because of my wonderful Jo.

Several station wagons would transport a few Seeing Eye Dogs and their blind masters to our area. Their dogs leading them door to door selling some very fine products. These dogs were trained in Rochester, a small town nearby. The blind young men and their wonderful dogs frequented the Three Sisters restaurant. Working around the house, I am on second shift, and wanting to save time, I would stop at the Three Sisters. It was such a pleasure to witness the joy they expressed and shared with all that were near.

Mary, the one and only waitress in this small restaurant, was such a joy to be around. Mary had an upbeat personality. When something was joyful she added to it. She would burst into the joy with whit and add her fun antics for all to hear. The owner was a fine chef and always keeping busy cooking and cleaning his kitchen that was out in the open. Frequenting this place, a couple of times a week I became a friend of his and I admired his love for his work.

This place had several booths along a wall and a counter you could also sit at. The drivers of the young men would sit at the counter and move back and forth to the booths to assist. Reading the menus and helping with the dogs, seeing all were happy. It was not just a restaurant now, it became a place of joy.

When the first blind man entered the establishment, Mary greeted him with, "I have a table with a view." The young blind man replied "You're looking your gorgeous self as always, Mary." The dog under the tables and the young men seated and talking about what a great day it was to be out in the fresh air.

One of the bosses who assisted was looking through the newspaper and called out Robert, "didn't you say, you were looking for a new bedroom set?" "Yes Frank, I have you found something for me?" Frank said, "I'll read you this ad that's in today's paper". "Beautiful *bedroom set, large bed, with two night stands, a dresser, with very large mirror and twin lamps, only $299.00." Robert quickly reported , "Call and find out the price without the mirror and two lamps." "You know, I am saving my money to renew my drivers license." "one of this blind friends remarked, "he's a much better driver than I." Each time I encountered these wonderful people I felt better from the experience. When I told my **Jo**, she would say how it helped her to know of the hardships that they could overcome.*

One day sitting next to one of the sighted leaders, I asked him what was the most outstanding story of this group he knew about. He told me the police were called to investigate a loud noise complaint. It was near midnight and they found, after a long time, to their surprise a blind man roofing his mother's house. It was a warm night and he didn't know the time. The police assisted him down, told him he should go to bed, but he replied, "Officer, I am not sleepy." Jo, would say, "It is so hard to stop these wonderful people , they are so special.

Wooden Phone Booth

We have Public Television – Channel 56 – in our area, which auctions off items each year. It's money they raise for local charity. I bought a Vernor's barrel one year; I hoped it would retain the Vernor's aroma, but it didn't. I tried for two years to get an old-time phone booth from them for our recreation room with no success.

I had talked at work about bidding unsuccessfully on the booth, when a friend told me that his daughter worked for the Phone Company. He said she would see what she could do. She found out it was against the law to buy old phone booths in Michigan, something to do with theft in old buildings, but that the phone company would sell to employees. Over 500 people were on the waiting list, including us. I never heard from them, unfortunately.

One day, **Jo** called me at work and told me to rush home – a phone booth was being delivered from Chicago. **Jo** said a friend had made some connections and had promised her one. I got home, and, sure enough, a truck came with two phone booths. I could choose the one I wanted. My remarkable **Jo** had come through again!

*I asked **Jo** why she hadn't told me about this before, and she said she wasn't sure about getting it and hadn't wanted to disappoint me if it hadn't happened. I assured **Jo** that she had never in her lifetime disappointed me.*

*The phone booth is approximately seven feet tall and two and half feet square. It has a fan, automatic lighting, and a very nice seat in it. Later, **Jo** ordered a pay phone from New York. It became a great asset to our recreation room. Old and young alike are excited about how it looks and works. You*

can have a private conversation when the door is closed, the bells ring when you insert the money, and the money is returned to you, no charge. What could be better?

I was so lucky to have **Jo** as my partner for life. She would think things out without telling you about it. **Jo** planned for success, then that success was shared. Now you know why I say, "**Remember my Jo**." God willing, she will call me on that phone. Her voice was always such a pleasure to hear.

Please phone me, Jo

Jo gave me everything I could desire
happiness, joy on our telephone wire
Her soft voice her sweet words so down to
earth
once again I thank God for her marvelous
birth.
To hear her voice
I would rejoice
She loved to talk
even as we walked
I'll take her voice any way I can
it was the way our love began
Hours on the phone, Jo never tired
"you be careful" I'd tease, "don't wear out the
wire"
She would laugh and say, "Aw Ken,"
take a breath and start again

Vincent

Nothing is more comforting than good neighbors. When the Vincents purchased the home next to us, they became very important to us from the first day we met. Our friendship increased when they came home with Diva and Laika, two adorable little dogs. **Jo** and I had the joy of playing with them anytime we wanted. Diva always ran to **Jo**, if I mentioned her name.

We were introduced to their family and friends at many of the wonderful parties they gave over the years. We attended their annual Christmas parties to benefit the Michigan Animal Rescue League that resulted in their taking a truckload of gifts to a shelter each year. Dr. Vincent, and his charming wife Kate, always brought us immense joy. Don Cherry, Kate's father, was so much fun. **Jo** and I always looked forward to the joy he brought others.

They took fantastic trips all over the world; Russia and the Ukraine, I think, was their first trip. They would scuba dive annually in the waters near Cozumel and Bonaire. They went on safari in Kenya a couple of times. Eddy took his mother once and she told me how proud she was of her son. Kate and Eddy were in the U.S.S.R. for the coup! They had no fear, but the scuba diving and the trips to foreign countries always worried me and **Jo**. Think of these fantastic trips – the Orient Express, a cruise in the Arctic Circle, Peru and Bolivia and the rain forest. They even went to Churchill, Manitoba to photograph polar bears that often stood a foot taller than they did. I know now that **Jo** and I lived exciting lives through them. When they write their book, be sure to read it.

I want to let people know how hard Kate and Eddy work and play. They are professionals at both often-working 18-hour days, *always helping others. I'm sure they both worked much too hard and never gave a thought to burn-out. In Heaven we want Kate and Eddy to be our neighbors, at a slower pace. I promise not to talk as much as I did here. I'll try to be more like my Angel **Jo**.*

No Joy Apart

I played baseball, football, basketball, golf, went fishing and bowling until I met **Jo**. We both liked sports, but only if we could enjoy them together. We bowled together when we were first dating. **Jo** was a good bowler – lady-like, very smooth and controlled, neat and clean.

Jo and I married, got good jobs and watched most of the sports on TV together. We had neighbors who raced cars and we enjoyed watching and being around them. Frieda raced Thunderbirds for Ford Motor Company.

I didn't realize until now that I never wanted to be away from **Jo**; we had to be together to enjoy anything. **Jo** went on a four-day trip to Florida with a cousin and two girl friends. With **Jo's** help, I made most of the arrangements, paid for the hotel, rented a car all in advance, and saw that **Jo** had plenty of cash, since credit cards hadn't come in to use yet. I wanted them to have a very good time with nothing to worry about. When **Jo** returned she said she had a fair time. She told me she missed me too much to have a good time.

We couldn't really enjoy anything if we were apart, not to the fullest. **Jo** and I both wanted this vacation to be great and we planned for it to be great, but it just didn't work. Before the plane took off in Florida, I was at the airport waiting for **Jo** in Detroit. I didn't want to be late to see my **Jo**.

Another time I remember **Jo** took her Mother to see her younger sister, Sharon, who was working for J.C. Penney's in New York City. It was their first plane trip. I never told **Jo** how I couldn't wait for her to return from that trip, too. I paid for the trip including two Broadway shows, "Fiddler on the Roof" and "Promises, Promises." **Jo** said it was as good as it could be without me. **Jo**, her Mother, and

Sharon always had fond memories of that visit. **Jo** *had a way of making all enjoy life.*

We were both dedicated to the other. We tried to have good times apart but it never worked for either of us. The few times we had to be apart, we did the best we could knowing that we would soon be together again. It was true love, no strings attached.

When I wake up with **Jo** *gone, the joy is gone out of everyday life. I ask for her help the first thing in the morning, I ask for her help the last thing each night, but the joy is gone. I love her so much; I miss her so much. My Angel being next to God will keep me on the right path.*

I try to eat and sleep, pay my bills, be as good a person as **Jo** *would want me to be, but it so hard to go on without her. I want to hear her name as before. It has been over a year, her monument ordered, but not in place. I put in a flowerbed of mostly white flowers; I do make a little progress with her help. I repaired something yesterday, but it was so hard without her.*

I was thinking of how she would have assisted me and the joy it would have been, hearing her encouragement as before, "Aw, Ken," once in a while. I never wanted her to work or do anything she didn't want to do. I only wish I could see her standing next to me. Why I am not with her this second only God knows.

Denise

Jo was so happy when her sister Irene told her that Denise, her first child, was on the way into this world. She knew that Irene and Chuck would take the greatest care of their children. **Jo** planned a shower and promised to be Denise's Godmother. She looked forward to this with great anticipation.

Den arrived on schedule; however, she had a hip displacement problem, which some children are born with. I believe it was Helen, Denise's Grandmother, who first discovered it. Irene was quick to jump in and with sacrifice and great care, set a record for a quick recovery for Den. **Jo** always credited Irene as being a super mother. The Doctor said he had never seen a child recover so fast and get the care that Irene had given Den. **Jo** and I couldn't have been more proud of anyone than we were of Denise. She was a beautiful child and a delight to be around.

Chuck and Irene were very very good parents, seeing to it that Denise had everything possible – plenty of love and a great education. They both devoted their lives to being good to Den. They proved that you could spoil her with luxuries and raise a wonderful girl. **Jo** and I were so thankful to have been around Denise while she was growing up. **Jo** was always showing pictures of Den, made scrapbooks, and we both went to every function that Den was a part of.

Denise graduated from Sterling Heights High School in 1976;

Irene and Chuck had the party in a hall, all the family was invited and everyone enjoyed themselves. **Jo** has an album of that affair. It is so nice to look back on. **Jo** is in Heaven remembering that wonderful day when the five ladies – **Jo**, Helen, Denise, Sharon, and Irene – had their picture taken together.

Chuck and Irene purchased a new Can-Am automobile for Denise that she used to drive back and forth to Central Michigan University in Mt. Pleasant. It was a one-of-a-kind automobile. **Jo** and I had the pleasure of seeing her many times there until she graduated in May of 1980. We had the graduation party at our home, while Irene and Chuck furnished everything and more.

Jo wanted the party to be perfect and she tried so hard; we got a tent set up, got a disc jockey, rented tables and chairs and decorated the garage with rolls of colored paper everywhere. The disc jockey would set up in the garage, the grownups would use the Recreation room with the Cheers bar and the dancing would be out on the driveway. The tent would allow for an overflow crowd.

Irene had sent out the invitations to friends and relatives all over the country and Chuck got all the

refreshments ordered. Den had about 50 friends coming from college and we had hoped for the one thing we couldn't order – that the weather would cooperate. Everything was set up the night before the party and looked so nice; however, it started to rain and rained for over 24 hours.

The party was to start at 6 p.m. We think everyone came with raincoats and umbrellas; we had to string lines to hold that gear. Raincoats were exchanged for several days. The garage couldn't be used; wind and rain stopped that. The disc jockey couldn't be used as planned. The tent came down, too much water.

Still the party was a success because of Irene, Chuck and ***Jo****. Denise had* ***Jo*** *join in dancing and singing school songs. The party lasted over 12 hours, good clean fun, a real celebration of Denise's accomplishments. Den has the pictures she can show you because of* ***Jo****. If you looked at the pictures* ***Jo*** *wanted everyone to see, you'd find pictures in an album that show everyone having a good time. The relatives still talk about that party.*

Mark, Denise's younger brother, should remember the party because of all the cars he parked. People coming and going in the heavy rain. He would take umbrellas to lead them into the house, park their cars, and then get the keys back to them.

Chuck will remember how he and a couple of his friends were bartenders at the Cheers bar. Chuck was at his best that night, a lot of fun with the young people and so proud of his daughter. Irene helped with everyone. Irene and **Jo** *had a wonderful time with all the relatives. It was a joy seeing Denise singing and dancing with all her friends. This was a party that Denise will never forget, if she will only take the time to reminisce.*

The party didn't turn out as we had planned, but as always Chuck, Irene and **Jo** *pitched in and some great, clean, enjoyable fun was had by all. Food, more than enough, drinks controlled plenty of it. No one was hurt, well over a hundred people, lots of talking and friendship. The Cheers bar; jukebox, pinball, slot machine, and phone booth got a good work out. The party broke up at 6 a.m. and our dog was happy about that.*

I'm sobbing now, wishing I could be with my **Jo** *to talk about the good time we had with Denise that night. I hope that we can relive the good times we had on earth. This would be one of the times I would like to relive.* **Jo** *and I looked at these pictures a lot. We took Den to Las Vegas after the party. Her Aunt Sharon joined us there and we all had a marvelous time.*

Mark

Mark's high school graduation in June 1979 was to be very special. Irene and Chuck planned and worked hard for the best possible graduation for both of their children. They got Mark a very special Z-28, one of the finest cars available then, as a graduation gift. **Jo** and I wanted to be a part of this marvelous day and offered our home for the party. She was so happy that this enjoyable event was happening and that we would be a part of it.

We all pitched in, looking forward to the open house for Mark. Irene sent out invitations, Chuck ordered the drinks, and **Jo** was involved in everything, ordering tables and chairs, the tent, and getting things ready in the house. She wanted everything done to perfection. There would be plenty of food and the bar was all set up, thanks to

Chuck. The weather was beautiful, too – pictures taken that day will show that. **Jo** made a special album that she always cherished. Mark had been a wonderful boy, and **Jo** and I were so proud of him. Mark was to join his father's company and, also, attend college.

The day of the party saw well over a 100 guests coming and going day and night. It was a fun time – music, dancing, singing, talking, and playing all the games – young and old. Relatives and friends came from all over the country. Mark always had a lot of friends, all very nice. **Jo** and I promised to take Mark to Las Vegas at a later date and we did. **Jo** never made a promise she didn't keep. I'm sure that **Jo** was the best aunt anyone could ever have. **Jo** prayed for Mark and his sister, Denise, and did everything she could for them.

Mark's party was a huge success, because of Irene, Chuck and my wonderful **Jo**.

Water and Gasoline

It was the fastest car we had ever owned. It ran like a rabbit and had been wonderful for several years. One day when I was driving to work, for some reason, it suddenly shut down. My heart started to race, but I managed, with great difficulties, to steer it off the expressway. It started up again when I tried the ignition, so I immediately set off in search of a gas station with a garage.

Over the course of the next few days, I did this several times. Each time they tried to fix it, I would pay for what they thought was wrong. It would run for a little while, then shut down as before. I would show the men at the new garage the bills I had already paid, so they wouldn't duplicate the repair, but then the car would quit again. Finally I left it for the day at a garage near work. I picked the car up after work and, once again, paid the repair bill. In the 20 miles it took to get home, the car was shutting down again. With **Jo's** help, I got it to another garage; this one was near home, and with repairmen I knew.

Later in the day the repairman called and said, "you can't run this fine machine on water." "What do you mean?" I asked. They couldn't believe that the car was running with over 10 gallons of water in the tank; neither could I! You know by now that **Jo** and I were loyal to the companies we worked for. Marathon employed me; consequentially, I used only their gas in our cars. I went back to the Marathon station where I had refueled last and told them about my car troubles. They said that a freak accident had allowed water to enter one of their tanks. They said they were truly sorry for my inconvenience and I was reimbursed for all my car repair bills.

A couple of weeks later, I came home a nervous wreck again. The car wasn't shutting down, but it was sure acting funny. **Jo** said, " I *love you, Ken, and I want you to get a new car. Your health is more important to me than money." "It'll be okay," I told her, but she insisted, "Please order a new car, Ken." I knew that* ***Jo*** *wanted what was best for both of us. I ordered a new Plymouth Roadrunner; in a very short time, I was feeling great about my car and those car repair troubles were a thing of the past. Once again,* ***Jo*** *cared more about me than I cared for myself. Again,* ***Jo*** *was right; she always had a magic touch to go along with her love.*

Jo's Uncle Jack

Jo's Uncle Jack was a very handsome man, married to a beautiful lady named Doris. In their younger years, they both aspired to be entertainers. They were show business personalities on the dance floor. Jack was a natural born Master of Ceremonies, always telling funny,

yet tasteful jokes, smoothly controlling any crowd. He always did a little entertaining; it was in his blood. Jack did go to Hollywood and had a couple of small parts in the movies, but I believe that Doris set her sights too high for both of them. It hurt her when they couldn't achieve those goals. You could see her physical beauty, but there was very little happiness showing in her lovely face.

Uncle Jack's full-time job was with a machinery and office moving company. It was sometimes very physical labor; however, when they moved offices, it was a lot easier on him. Whenever his work took him near **Jo's** office, he would stop in to see her. She would come home that night very happy and full of news, because they so enjoyed seeing each other. Still, I would say we only saw him ten times in fifty years. Each time was more than joyous. We attended a New Year's Eve party one year at their home and had an amazing time. He always danced with **Jo** and it made me so happy to see them smiling and having so much fun.

Jack and Doris had a small home in Michigan, but spent most of the year in Florida where he played golf year round. We knew that golf and the county club lifestyle was what he really enjoyed in the years after he retired.

The last time we saw Jack, he said someone had broken into his garage. Some tools had been stolen and their value for this insurance claim was placed at $995.00 Wouldn't you know it, his insurance company informed him that he had a $1,000.00 deductible! "That got a hearty laugh from us." I'm not sure if this was true, or just one of his many jokes; he had a million of them in his collection.

I wish we could have spent more time on earth with Uncle Jack, but maybe he will M.C. some joyous times in Heaven one day. **Jo** and I would like that very much. It's said that God grants all of our desires and that would be one of ours.

Amish

Irene and Chuck has a hunting place near Clare, Michigan; a big plus is that there is an Amish settlement in the area. Clare is a beautiful town and the Amish adds to its natural charm. I don't profess to know much about the Amish, only what I observed and later learned from books and a video I obtained from my local library. The video and some of the books were about the Pennsylvania Amish and so does not apply to all Amish communities.

Chuck likes to drive the back roads of Clare to look at the farms and the animals. At different times, we would see several buggies on their way to a different house for a special service held every two weeks. The horse-drawn buggies, all black, had windows that were so clean, everything so well-taken-care-of, with nothing out of place. The parents and the children would be sitting upright in the buggies, intent on where they were headed, dressed in clothes of their own making in the same simple style. We never went into an Amish house or farm, but they take such good care of everything one can pick them out from a distance. Their farms, horses, barns and houses are very plain and yet very beautiful. There would always be children playing in the yards, so happy and orderly.

Whenever we observed these lovely people in the modern world of shopping, their serenity and calmness was almost unbelievable. We encountered them mainly in supermarkets, hardwares and feed stores. One fall day, I went into a feed store with Chuck to buy feed for the deer and birds. Whenever we had the station wagon or the truck, he would buy the feed by the 100-lb bags, usually 5 to 10 bags at a time. He bought carrots and turnips for the deer, too. I was near the rear of the store when I saw a nine or ten-year-old Amish girl walking next to her father. She was the purest child I'd ever seen. I knew from the shyness in each step she took that her father, in that moment, was her entire world. I don't have words for how heavenly that sight was to me.

After a day spent in town among the Amish, Chuck and I would tell Irene and **Jo** that we were going to get a stretch Limousine Amish buggy with a race horse to pull it and we'd set the two of them in the back. It was a joke we liked to talk about. I could see the love **Jo** had for that lifestyle, so clean, neat, and calm. **Jo** always loved good, so she couldn't help but love these joyous people. She asked me questions about them I couldn't answer, so we both got books out of the library to learn more about the Amish way of life.

I loved the way **Jo** and I were raised, but when something like that little girl's love for her father stood out so pure, it made me stop and think. How proud that father was and how happily that little girl was twinkling. I told **Jo** about that little girl and how I wished she could have seen her.

I read that the Amish don't have mirrors and will not look at their reflections in store windows or objects. I can't think of anything now, even the Amish, without thinking of **Jo**; my reference was and always will be **Jo**. She couldn't survive without looking in the mirror several times a day. It wasn't to admire herself, but to be sure her hair and clothes were exact, so she would look nice at all times. God made all of us, but how we turned out, following the example set by our parents, is our choice. God, I am sure, was delighted at how both that little girl and **Jo** turned out. I know that there was not one day on this earth that I wasn't proud of my **Jo**. I always acted in a way that **Jo** could say the same of me.

Jo Loved Arrows

When you see an arrow, think of my wonderful **Jo**. The quills and shafts come in such beautiful colors, so she started using them as decorations. You don't buy the points, so they are not dangerous; **Jo** never wanted anything dangerous. She first saw them at Jay's, a sporting goods store up North, less than a mile outside of Clare. People come from all over the country to shop at this super-market-like sportsman's shop. Archery, fishing, guns, knives; everything for outdoors, even an indoor archery range. Chuck took us to Jay's at least 100 times. It is worth seeing, but plan to be there for several hours.

When **Jo** saw the arrows, she immediately found a beautiful new use for them. She put them in flowerpots to hold the flowers in place, as decorations in the yard, flowerbeds, recreation room, our garage and even in our spa room. You just stick them in the dirt and your job is done. They are a beautiful decoration and give the vines support. We put some away, because we didn't want to overdo it. **Jo** always had good taste, the best in my opinion.

She was selective in the colors and arrangements of these arrows, but still she found a great number of uses for them in and around our home. She loved the beauty they would add to anything. I have too many around now, but I can't help myself. I can't get too much of her; I think you understand. For me the arrows are a tribute to my **Jo**; I want everyone to **Remember my Jo**, so when you see a beautiful arrow think of my **Jo**. I purchased 40 of them and gave them to friends, neighbors, and relatives in memory of her. She was my Angel and I miss her so much. If you will **remember my Jo**, I will get to be with her in Heaven, which is my last goal in life.

Caroline

One day **Jo** came home from work all excited. She said she had heard we, as weekend -Foster Parents, could take some children home from the Sarah Fisher Home for Children. **Jo** asked me if I would help her. **Jo** asked for so few things that I jumped at the chance to help. We went to the home to see what we needed to qualify – a tour of our home, church, and some interviews and a certificate from our doctor stating we were in good physical health.

In a very short time we were introduced to a lovely sister, a nun at the home. Sister Louise was elderly and sweeter than her age. Each time

we saw her it was our pleasure. **Jo** took Sister Louise to St Owens Church. Sister Louise checked out our home and was equally impressed. She assigned us four teenagers for some time. She called one day excited and wanting to see us as soon as possible. She had a three-year-old named Caroline she wanted us to take. We were both over 40 and thought we were too old for Caroline, but we knew we would be good to her and she would be good for us. We told Sister Louise about our feelings. She insisted we give it a try, so we did.

On the weekends, **Jo** took Caroline everywhere – shopping, the beauty shop, had her nails done in clear polish. Caroline fell in love with

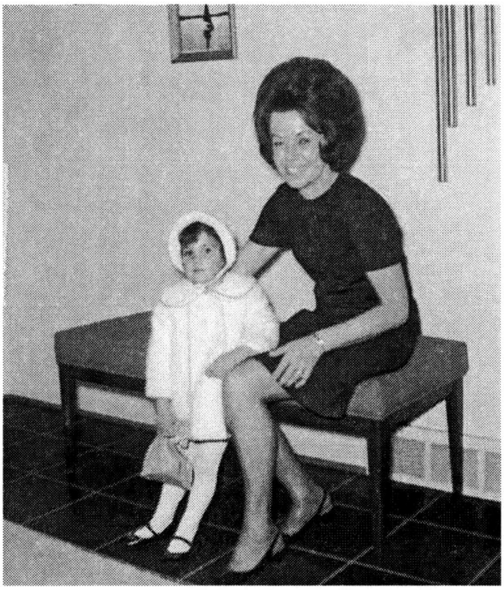

Jo in a very short time – new outfits, lots of toys, a normal family life, getting into food preparation, dinner, walking the dog, visiting our relatives. Caroline liked to go places, riding in the car, going to the mall. Like all little children I've known she played one against the other. If **Jo** said "No," she would come to me and vice versa.

All the time we spent with Caroline was wonderful, but the time came when she didn't want to return to the home. We had been instructed that if that happened – and it always does – we would have to walk away. **Jo** and I often talked about the good experience we had and wondered how Caroline was doing, but when you made that kind of a disconnection you had to stay away for the good of the child. She was our last weekend Foster child. Life has its good times; it's impossible to comprehend why they have to end. **Jo** was always my good times and I don't understand why that had to end. Some have told me I will get the answer in Heaven. When **Jo** entered Heaven it became a better place. That's why I want to be with my **Jo** as soon as possible.

Jo and Jury Duty

I am not sure now what year this happened, but I do know the story. It was when **Jo** was called for Jury Duty. **Jo** was such a wonderful person that I always tried to shield her from being hurt emotionally, but I couldn't shield her from Jury Duty. She wanted to serve and be a good citizen, but hoped she wouldn't be put in a position to decide a close judgment. She never wanted to hurt anyone. It happened to be a murder case, open and shut. A southern white boy killed an elderly black man over a parking space. The elderly black man was a good man and had no blame whatsoever and had pleaded for his life before he was shot dead.

The boy came to court very nicely dressed, a handsome young fellow, but there were numerous witnesses who had seen him kill the black man in broad daylight. He got the maximum sentence. **Jo** pondered over why something like this could happen in this wonderful world where so many good things can be done; what a shame that some one would do a thing like that. **Jo** felt so bad, because none of this should have happened. I had no answer for her.

Sometime later **Jo** was called up for another murder case; this time drug use was involved. Once again she was seeing the bad side of this world. She couldn't believe that these seemingly nice young girls had had their lives here on earth destroyed by drugs. The girls were not on trial, but **Jo's** feelings for them and what they could have accomplished she expressed to me each night when she returned home from court. The young girls brain had been fried from using drugs. They didn't know their names. Again she asked me why. I told her the girls just got on the wrong path; together we felt so sad about this.

Try each day to make the world a better place as **Jo** did. Don't hurt anyone and stay away from harmful drugs. Maybe if they had read

Remember My Jo, *and drawn the proper life lessons from it, those young people may have been saved with no trials necessary.* ***Jo*** *always kept me on the right path from the day I met her. I know from looking back that my life was wonderful because of* ***Jo***. *When we are together again, it will be even better with my Angel* ***Jo***.

Kidney Stone

We are about fifty-five years old and are both still working. It had been a very good day, **Jo** was with me and I was with **Jo**. What could be better? We retired to bed as usual and all was right with the world. Suddenly, I woke up from a sound sleep at 3 a.m. because I was hurting. I was in more pain than I ever imagined possible. I crawled into the bathroom and was very, very sick. **Jo** woke up and seeing the bathroom light on, gently asked what she could do for me? I told her I would be better in a little while, thinking it couldn't get worse; boy, was I wrong!

Jo called the local police department for help and soon a very tall policeman, so gentle and kind, showed up at our door. He said I would need an ambulance to get me to the hospital right away. He assured **Jo** that he would help lock up the house and assist us in any way that he could. **Jo** followed the ambulance to the hospital, then called her sister, Irene, who, at the proper time, called our work places and told them we wouldn't be in. **Jo** had everything under control.

I got wonderful treatment in the hospital for a week, then was sent home to try and pass what turned out to be a very large, barbed kidney stone. After failing to pass the stone in the allotted time, I went back into the hospital. This time I got the worse treatment anyone could imagine. I had a wonderful surgeon, thank God, and I'm sure he saved my life, but these nurses and orderlies were very different from the first group. After a few days of them, I tried to escape in the middle of the night in the pouring down rain. I made it past the nurse's desk, down the elevator, and across the lobby to the front entrance. I was captured by two burly security guards that escorted me back to my bed and that poor group of incompetent nurses and orderlies. I could write a horror story about the medical care I got during the rest of my stay.

As always **Jo** did everything possible to insure my comfort. She went to work, but checked up on me via telephone whenever she could, and saw me as much as the hospital would allow. In the meantime, she kept a 6-hour dental appointment that had been prearranged for Saturday, took care of the house, dog, bills, and cars by herself. She arranged for my return home after the operation and gently nursed me back to health. If I had had three good wives, they couldn't have done as much as **Jo** alone did for me.

I often thanked **Jo** for what she'd done for me then and I'm thanking her again. It was 14 years later when she herself received poor medical care at the same hospital and, unfortunately, didn't survive. She had good treatment on minor problems there, but they helped her not a bit with her major medical crisis. I want to thank those who did their best to help her. If she had been your nurse, you would have remembered my **Jo**, because she would have given you so much love and devotion.

Someday in the future

When you don't think death will happen for a long time, you put some things off till later. **Jo** was retired for 5 years before me; because she took an early retirement. We strolled through life together and it was such a pleasure knowing that we could enjoy each day. That was the plan. We had prepared the big things, so as not to be a burden to anyone. Looking and thinking of the good times ahead, we had everything taken care of for the next ten years. I told **Jo** we will look at everything when we get old. I wasn't thinking clearly; **Jo** would never get old to me.

We planned to someday take the time out of our daily lives to read the 2000 plus letters we had saved from our World War 11 correspondence. We would read the mush we wrote, discuss it, laugh, cry, and reminisce. Some questions would be asked and answered; it would all be in fun, with a great deal of love.

We planned to go back to Potawatomi, the place where we spent our honeymoon, walk the grounds, and drive through the country like we did so many years before. See if any of our love was still there. Look at the lake, stars and the moon. We waited too long.

Thousands of pictures would be looked at with less haste than before. We would take the hours and hours necessary to watch our videos. We wanted to talk about some of her things, how she took care of them, what they meant to her; some gifts, who they came from; that would have been such a joy.

Being near her, asking her silly questions that she would be sure to answer with a great deal of love, always wanting to hear, "Aw, Ken," was what I was always waiting for. If the world would slow down, we would step off together. It just slowed down for my **Jo**. I want it to slow down for me.

I miss my Jo

*I miss the presence of my **Jo**, even though she's everywhere for me. How can this be? It's called memories. I can't think of a single thing that didn't involve her. Over 55 years of being together, our lives*

*were intertwined. We had work, play, joy, sorrow, fast, slow, storms, calm, hot, cold, day, night, good, bad, dirty, clean, wet, dry, up, down, and around. When you have done it all there's nothing more left to do. I feel **Jo** and I did it all and had it all. We had pluses and minuses; but the pluses won out 1000 to 1 because of my wonderful **Jo**.*

Our dream was to have love, health, happiness, progress, and a wonderful relationship on our journey through life. The journey was smooth and comfortable most of the way. The view was scenic and colorful; it was safe and enjoyable.

We did a lot of planning; put a lot of effort into each project we wanted to complete. We looked for property for over two years. We designed our home with features that are still outstanding 30 years later. With our devotion to each other, work, and planning, we were able to afford the new products that came on the market. ***Jo*** *was instrumental in every phase of our projects.*

Automatic this, automatic that, television, computers, air travel, things that kings and queens didn't have when we were born. Marvelous things we couldn't imagine. Just think of the magnificent life we lived, add the love of my wonderful ***Jo*** *and I want to thank God that we had it all for over 50 years. Then I'm looking forward to eternity with my* ***Jo****.*

She wanted progress and always wanted things better for everyone. It was my desire for ***Jo*** *to enjoy everything she could want or think of.* ***Jo's*** *desires became my ambition to please. Oh, if you could have known my* ***Jo*** *the way I did, you would have wanted to please, as I did.* ***Jo*** *would look over everything and give me an, "aw Ken," with a little laugh. Do you remember what* ***Jo*** *was saying to me? It was, "I love you, Ken." I will* ***remember my Jo*** *forever.*

Jo's Retirement Gift

Jo and I knew that retirement wasn't for everyone, so all I can do is write about our experience. At one time corporations set up a "30 and out" pension plan to help ease the older workers out and help the young enter the work force. We had pension plans at Chrysler and the Teamsters that would begin at some unspecified date in the future, so we made plans for that day. We were both proud of our productivity all our working lives and hoped we would be well enough to produce until our retirements. We looked forward to a good retirement, but a lot of people don't make it, because they think they have to work until they can't get out of bed anymore. In our situation, we wanted our time of leisure to be spent together. I was so happy if I could be with Jo and she felt the same about me.

Retirement came to **Jo** quite suddenly, because of Chrysler Corporation's financial problems. The day they offered her an early retirement, she called me at work to discuss it; I said that it sounded excellent and she should consider taking it. She brought home the papers, we went over them together, and she retired the next day.

At that time I only had 19 years in with the Teamsters, so I felt I should stay a little longer. After 5 more years of steady work, I called Lowell, our financial advisor, who kept me under lock and key, and gave him all of our holdings. After I had answered all his questions, I asked, "can I afford to retire?" Lowell said, "you and **Jo** have done very well and I can see no reason for you to keep working if you want to retire." **Jo** was in full agreement. We rolled over our accounts, keeping Lowell, and the two other brokers we already had, very busy. At **Jo's** request, I saw that they both got some added accounts as well.

Having our brokers in our home several times after we retired was a must. Knowing Mark A. Rhodes (Merrill Lynch) was such a pleasure and Thomas G. Marzonie (Smith Barney) always had our financial affairs on his front burner. The day they met **Jo** everything they did for us was a win-win situation. They made money in the stock market for us and became lifetime friends. They were three phenomenal men to be associated with. They all told me they will never forget **Jo**.

This didn't just happen, mind you; we had prepared for it by making wise financial decisions all our lives. The day we were both retired; we began to live the same lifestyle, still putting money in the bank each year. We read articles, sent away for booklets, and sought out assistance from banks and brokers; we looked into anything we thought would assist us to live better. We endeavored to live within our means, not above or below. If we wanted something special, we would save our money until we could afford it. Sometimes it meant seeking out new investments.

You remember how **Jo** invested successfully in a new stock when we wanted to purchase a bigger television?

We never wanted to be a burden to anyone or seek out things we couldn't afford. We had our hands in everything by our own desire. We drew up the plans for our house searched out the property on our own, and painted, washed walls, cleaned carpets, stained floors and furniture ourselves. We got an Ironrite, so **Jo** could do our ironing and pressing; we only sent out the things we felt could be done better by somebody else. **Jo** worked hard, always bought quality clothes and appliances and took great care of them. If I had the time, I changed the oil in our cars. In the long run, we had excellent things for many years. After they had served us well, we would put them out to pasture.

All these things were done before retirement, so we could retire and leave the heavy work to others. In retirement our cars would be full-service, our house would be painted and repaired, our lawn cut, trees would be taken care of and fertilized, and snow removal would be done under contract. Any other time-consuming job would be for other people to do.

We took time to smell the roses and to hang plants around the yard; time to have things to play with, as well as time to play. We had time together in the glider, time together to listen to music. We went shopping together when we wanted to. There would be no more rushing around to someone else's schedule. We went to the dentist at 9 a.m. and ate out whenever we wanted to, always together.

Each day we asked if we could be of help to the other. Breakfast, lunch and dinner were prepared together. We made the beds together and helped each other with the washing. If anything was broken, we both jumped in to fix it. We spent over ten contented years of retirement together; wonderful, marvelous years being with each other day and night.

*We talked about our future as if we would live forever. Statistics said that women outlived men by several years, so I made financial plans with the idea that **Jo** would outlive me. **Jo** would say, " we should leave this world for Heaven together," and I always made the joke that if the world would slow down, we would step off together. The world slowed down for **Jo**, because she was hurting and she stepped off; I wanted to go with her, but this was not to be. Now I just want it to slow down for me. Until it does, I'll always be "Remembering my **Jo**." I've read that God always has a better plan for you than you can imagine. I know now that we will have everything we ever wanted, and more, in our future life with God. I know **Jo** is waiting for me; I'm on my way, bringing my unending love and devotion.*

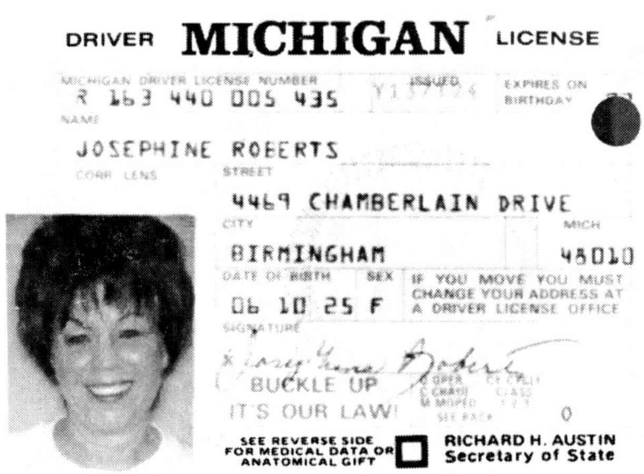

DRIVER **MICHIGAN** LICENSE

MICHIGAN DRIVER LICENSE NUMBER
R 163 440 005 435
ISSUED
EXPIRES ON BIRTHDAY
NAME
JOSEPHINE ROBERTS
CORR LENS
STREET
4469 CHAMBERLAIN DRIVE
CITY
BIRMINGHAM
MICH
48010
DATE OF BIRTH SEX
06 10 25 F
IF YOU MOVE YOU MUST CHANGE YOUR ADDRESS AT A DRIVER LICENSE OFFICE
SIGNATURE
BUCKLE UP
IT'S OUR LAW!
SEE REVERSE SIDE FOR MEDICAL DATA OR ANATOMICAL GIFT
RICHARD H. AUSTIN
Secretary of State

Guess Jo's age in this picture.
Answer on last page.

Jo and Easter

Easter was very important to **Jo**, a time to look her very best. She felt she had to look as good as possible in the house of the Lord. **Jo** honored her church by the clothes she wore. She never said this, but it was evident in her preparation. In her youth, hats were the rage. She didn't have a lot of hats, but each one was specially chosen. You could see her blue eyes would sparkle and shine as she put each one on. I loved every hat **Jo** picked out..

High-heel shoes were a must to look dressed up. I can't watch an old movie and see the ladies dressed up that I don't think of **Jo**. I sometimes think of her dressing up as really dressing down, because she never wore too much of anything – just the right amount. She liked a bracelet-watch not a bracelet and a watch. She wore rings on one finger only. **Jo** always took time to look elegant, not flashy. She wanted people to glance at her not look at her. Still I always felt that the men looked at **Jo** and the women glanced at her.

Jo talked favorably of anyone who was trying to improve themselves. She never wanted anyone to slide back. **Jo** and I were especially blessed at Easter and the rest of each year I had with her. We enjoyed so much of life together.

Jo won't honor St. Owen this year, because she is in Heaven. I'm sure God will see that she is happy on this day. This important place, St. Owen, that **Jo** looked so beautiful in won't see her. I have memories of how she looked, how she prepared, how her blue eyes would sparkle.

Her hair being done, her shoes polished and so clean, her dress so neat and nothing out of place, her famous hats, **Jo** primping in front of the mirror, the smile I would see because she was so happy. **Jo** would be sure to clean her diamond rings and ask me to look at them to make sure she had done a good job.

I always told **Jo** how proud I was of her. She would say, with a little laugh "Aw, Ken, I can't look good all the time." I would say, "I can't ever remember when you didn't look good. You do your hair before you go to the beauty parlor and if we have trouble with the TV, you clean it before the repairman comes." She laughed at that.

I love my **Jo** so much and this first Easter in over 50 years, without her hurts too much for me to know how to explain it to anyone. I sob a lot, I'm extremely emotional, the front of my brain hurts and hurts. I don't understand why my heart doesn't break.

Jo was my life; and I want to be with her again. I remembered **Jo**, because she always said; "I'm

*yours and you're mine forever and ever." **Jo** never told me anything that wasn't true. It makes me so sad that **Jo** is not here for Easter, for me to see God's creation in the flesh. I always ask **Jo** to help me through these hard times and she always does. **Jo** and I will do great in Heaven. I hope very soon. Easter was always such a pleasure when **Jo** was with me. I look forward to being with **Jo**.*

Jo's hats were never a chance selection
they showed her desire for perfection
The time she took was never hid
she was proud of everything she did
Jo would put forth the effort late into the night
nothing thrown together, she took the time to make it right
Never complaining or explaining
with that gleam in her eye
Jo was high in the sky
Nothing could interfere with her going
she felt it a pleasure just to enter St. Owens.

Tell Me What to Do

When you're friendly, kind, and caring, you bring a glow that helps to light the world. **Jo** did that for me all the time. I was never in the dark when she was with me. I'm mourning my **Jo** now; it's something I couldn't prepare for. I surely never wanted it; it hurts too much. I'm told I have got to get over my grief at Jo's sudden passing. It's been suggested how, but none of the suggestions have worked for me. I have tried to no avail.

My sanctuary is our home where we spent most of our lives together; so many wonderful memories of **Jo** are here. It hurts me, but it gives me comfort. Somehow, looking at the wonderful things **Jo** was involved in reinforces my love for her.

Until I am with my wonderful **Jo**, this is what I want–my sanctuary and the memories of the beautiful life **Jo** and I had together. I have tapes of **Jo's** voice – not enough, video tapes, seldom of her alone, – not enough; pictures old and new – not enough, material possessions that she loved – not enough, never enough to bring back the happiness we shared. I know **Jo** has her memories with her. We have to get together and put those memories with mine. I speak to **Jo** and God every day and night, asking them to help me.

Relatives, friends, and the clergy tell me I have things to do before I leave this world. I have asked God to tell me what they are. I know **Jo** is an angel, so I ask God to send her down to tell me. I'll do anything to be with my wonderful **Jo** once again.

When I heard so many say that I still have something left to do, I had a trust set up. That wasn't it, or I wouldn't still be here. The only thing I can think of is to tell about my life with my wonderful **Jo**. It's the only thing that I can give of importance that I have not accounted for. I have been asking for help, so I could give **Jo's** memories justice. It would give me great pleasure to tell the good things I enjoyed in life because I shared them with my **Jo**.

Heaven

I have had a lot of time to think now that **Jo** is not with me as she was for so many years. I know she is still with me, but I can no longer see her in the earthly way. Since she departed from my sight, my first wish is that we were back together at the prime of our lives.

I guess love should never be divided. It has to be all encompassing. I want **Jo** and me to be with everyone we loved. I wonder how many humans have written these same words. The mystery of life on this planet, I guess, must remain a mystery; surely I can't change that and shouldn't try. I can only make references to things I can know here on Earth. I'm sure God has a better plan, but I want my desires known. They comfort me now.

First, I would embrace my **Jo**, then my mother and father. I never want any of us to feel disconnected again. I know there were times when **Jo** and I were so happy we wanted that time to last forever. I'm sure heaven will hold that for us, too. I started to write this and now I have gotten myself into a corner as we say here on Earth. I believe that in Heaven there will be no corners to paint yourself into or out of. I will be with my astonishing and beautiful **Jo** in a loving circle that never ends. I want that as soon as possible.

Eternal Circle

On June 10, 1925, something very, very, special happened for me – **Jo** was born. It would be approximately 16 years later that love at first sight would invade my life. I wasn't looking for a girlfriend that wonderful day; it started out like any other. Then we met, a meeting that would last forever, because of **Jo**. **Jo** came from another state; I must have been waiting for her. I made a trip of three blocks, hadn't planned it, it just happened. **Jo** had come hundreds of miles for us to meet. It became my desire to make that trip worth her effort.

I wanted to make the rest of her journey here on earth as easy and joyous as possible. Love flourished for both of us. **Jo's** love touched everyone, especially our family. Mother and Dad loved her beyond belief.

Jo or I had no control over our first years on earth; once we were married our plans became one. It was never what I wanted or she wanted, it was what we wanted. I know we were overprotective of each other, but we wanted it that way.

Fifty years together set no records, but my love for **Jo** did set a record that will last for eternity. Great men climb mountains reaching for the top. I look for my great glory with my **Jo** in the eternal circle. That embrace with **Jo** will put an end to this life; God will put us together again forever, and our love will flourish.

I was told to write my memories of **Jo** and that if I could make you **remember my Jo**, I could again be with her. In my stories about **Jo** you know that white and clean always pleased her. I special-ordered white flowers for the anniversary of her birth. I know that **Jo** was an angel for me. You might not understand this, but until I'm with her, I'll miss the love she gave me and the pleasure in the nearness of her.

Sometimes the sky lights up in a storm and the rain on the roof has a gentle clicking drum beat. Cloudy, dark skies were no match for my **Jo**. When I was with **Jo**, the sun would soon slip through. The beautiful blue sky, soft white clouds I knew were near. The gentle clicking rain was music to my ears and no harm was in the air, if I could hold my **Jo**.

We embraced each other and the future. The rain, as always, predicted wonderful growth in our relationship if **Jo** was near. Love always grew at a faster rate from the cleansing of the rain. When I enter those white clouds, we will be together; the fear of storms will end forever in our eternal embrace.

I want my Jo to watch over me
want her to see
that we will be
together for eternity
My book was written to tell the world
what a good part of her life was like
How God would approve of her kindness,
her devotion and her always being polite
Jo going first was unthinkable to me
in heaven that couldn't be
Please God put us together for eternity
God in heaven only knows how long I have to go
before I'm united with lovable, wonderful Jo.

Fantasize

My wonderful life on this Earth started with my Mother and Dad. When **Jo** came into my life, they embraced her as lovingly as they had me. The four of us had a brief time together, but it was Heaven on Earth. Then Mother died, then Dad, and then **Jo**. I'm the only one left on this Earth and only God knows why. I don't want to dishonor my life, so each day I ask for help. I ask Mother, Dad, **Jo** and God to help me keep on keeping on, but my real wish if truth be told, is to join them as soon as I can.

Sometimes, in my mind, I go back and change my Mother's passing. I write the story the way that I would have wanted it. In this version of our story, Mother gets well and together we do all of the things Dad, **Jo** and I did. The most important thing in this fantasy is that Mother is now with us sharing in our happiness. We are happy talking every night, helping each other, as everyone's love for one another keeps growing. I see us all working together, **Jo** in the middle of everything, each improving on what the other wants. I see Mother making **Jo** even more beautiful, **Jo** doing the same for Mother, each trying to out-do the other, always with great tenderness. I imagine the future and joy those two could have created by assisting Dad and me to be a force for even more love.

I think of the trips **Jo** and I took, the one to Florida and each one thereafter. Mother would have had her welcome input; oh, the joy she and **Jo** would have had in the planning of hair-do's, clothing, and all the other refinements. I think of the joy of our new house and all the fine people we got to know over the years. Mother and **Jo** could have shared all the progress we made. If it's true that the more loved ones you share with the greater the joy, then Mother, Dad, **Jo** and I would have had Heaven here on Earth.

*Mother never learned to drive. She didn't want to. **Jo**, always wanting to help in any way she could, would drive mother any place she wanted to go any time of the day or night. The two of them sharing in what they could do was love at its best – Mother taking care of **Jo's** hair and beauty, something she loved to do, and **Jo** driving Mother where she needed to go, a thing **Jo** loved to do. If my fantasy had come true, this would have made the two luckiest husbands on this Earth even happier.*

*With Mother still with us, the grass would have been greener, the sky bluer, the fragrance of flowers even stronger. Each day would have been filled with rapture for all. Everything would have been improved beyond belief. Mother could have been the spice of our lives. I could name a million reasons why I wanted Mother to stay with us, but love was the main reason. Now that **Jo** has left me to join Mother and Dad in Heaven, I want to go back in time and be able to drive up to the marquee at the Broadway Capital Theater, sound the musical horns, and have **Jo** walk towards me looking so beautiful. I want to drive her home to Mother and Dad and live happily ever after. I hope this is the plan God has for me, that I live out my fantasy; until then, I will always **remember my Jo** and be happy that she is with Mother and Dad.*

Jo for me, Leta for Dad
so much love we did have
Two couples consisting of
four people in love
Knowing it was all
blessed from above
A fantasy for only a few years
parting, we shed many tears
They have seen what I'm going to see
the three in heaven waiting for me
God knows the future I've been told
the fantasy I want, for now, is on hold.

By Example

It is my wish to leave this world a better place than I entered. The stories I write about, I believe, enable me to do just that. I hope your reading of them will assist you in achieving the same goal. It's said, " the journey of a thousand miles begins with a single step." I add to that, "it has to be in the right direction to have any meaning." I'm sorry to say that what I see and hear on this earth today is often in the wrong direction. I know that there are some wonderful people on this earth, who want what we all want – peace, love, and happiness.

At the famous fork in the road, you must take the road for good and never cross over. What I would like to see is smut, dope, profanity, graffiti, blight and theft eradicated. I'd like to see all people helping, not hurting, what God created. Taking care of yourself and those around you is a good start; being a good person means that others are free to do the same. It is important to set a good example. **Jo** did that for me; she helped me everyday of my life. It wasn't ever forced upon me. **Jo's** gentle instruction was always in the right direction.

What a wonderful start in life I had – wonderful, loving parents to start my life, **Jo** for the rest of my life, and memories of her even now. **Jo** was always wanting good to flourish, moving in the right direction, and always walking away from the bad. Too much of anything on earth is bad, except love. Credit, gambling, leisure, and savings; these top the list of things you can have too much of, but you can never have too much love. Love equals kindness, friendliness, cleanliness, tenderness, and kinship. My Mother, Dad, and **Jo** gave me all their love.

Good, honest, hard work is necessary on this earth. Set high goals and ask that those around you do the same. **Jo** and I voted in most elections, never giving the City, State or Federal Government even a *small problem. If someone you know has broken trust don't defend them, just look for, and give, a better person a chance. Never hurt anyone, surround yourself with good people, and enjoy your life. Let people know that your life was good, because of their being around you and you around them. There are wonderful people who can make this a better world. Give the good people who are next in line a chance.*

Can we forgive the others? Certainly, then pass them by for the ones who are more deserving. Always look for the good, walk away from the bad. ***Jo*** *made this a better place by the ethical code she adhered to. Now she graces Heaven.*

Wedding Anniversary

It was nearing our Fiftieth wedding anniversary and the question had to be asked, even though the answer was already known.

"**Jo**, what can I get you?" I asked.

"Ken, I've got everything I want," **Jo** always answered. She had a huge supply of Estee Lauder products. They were her favorites. The fragrance was fantastic and was the right mix for her. She always received complements. When Estee Lauder Company issued stock on the New York exchange, I called one of my brokers to purchase several shares for my **Jo**. When the day came, I told her she had enough Estee stock to take a bath in her most desired perfume. She said, "Aw, Ken," with a little laugh. That secret phrase meant, "I love you, Ken."

Jo knew I watched the television program "Cheers" a lot and liked an episode about a Karaoke machine. I told her about that being something I would be interested in the future. I was sure it would be an asset for our recreation room; as well as being able to sing along and record with famous entertainers, it had some very nice features, such as a microphone with which you could also make announcements. That was the gift she gave me.

We both liked our gifts. **Jo** told me she was so happy about her Estee Lauder gift, making me happy, too. I purchased some recording tapes for my Karaoke machine and we planned on using them in the future. I'm sorry to say we didn't get a chance to, since **Jo** passed away so unexpectedly, so the joy was only in the planning. We will recreate our plan at a later date.

Jo and I always had everything we desired. It was marvelous to live that way. Having **Jo** as my wife for so many years made most *things possible. We will some day resume our singing and will spread the Estee fragrance around Heaven, which is a better place because of my **Jo**.*

With an ad in her hand, she wanted to
shop
we headed for the mall, our very first stop
Estee Lauder was first on her list
what was good for Jo, I would never resist?
Jo loved Estee Lauder
the perfume I had bought her
A fragrance so rare
none could compare
Knowing the product around her
she always stopped at their counter
Jo would always buy
with that gleam in her eye
"It's for you, Ken, I wear it,"
I was happy to share it
All those who walked by got a whiff
I'm sure you're getting my drift.

Sobbing and Tears

I was walking in our yard yesterday; it would have been our 51st. Wedding anniversary. We have a group of lilac bushes; with the damp morning air and just a slight wind, the smell was like it must be in Heaven. Whenever I feel something special, I talk to my **Jo**. For some reason, I feel she hears me better in the house. When I stepped into the house, I said, "**Jo**, the fragrance of the lilacs is so marvelous, it's like your being around." With **Jo** in the car or passing me in the hall, there was a hint of "Estee Lauder," so special, so phenomenal. That bouquet was present only for me from **Jo**, no one else had it.

Nothing could fulfill me more than my **Jo**. I hurt so much now; I've told my friends and relatives that all I can think of now is **Jo**. They loved her very, very much I know, who wouldn't? To know her was to love her. There are famous songs, poems, letters, books, and movies – all about love – and they all remind me of her.

Remembering **Jo** is what I do. Sobbing and tears want to start. Why must the love I have for her rise to sobbing and tears? It's the loss of **Jo**, thinking of and caring so much for her, grieving that she is gone from me.

I was never a hard person, but this has made me emotional to a degree that is very uncomfortable for me. I know **Jo** doesn't want me to be like this, but I can't stop it. Sobbing and tears well up in me, it hurts so much, and moves to the front of my head, throbbing. I ask **Jo** to help me until it goes away, but it was never meant for **Jo** and I to be apart.

If an accomplished songwriter had **Jo** as his inspiration, knew **Jo** the way I did, he would write the most beautiful song on earth. If only I had the genius of a great poet, a writer, or a movie producer; still, I'll do the best I possibly can, so you, too, will **remember my Jo**.

Jo Would Let You Know

In this world you are sure to come across someone who will not do his share. The Peter Principle talks about people who rise to a level where they can't function, but they will not step down. **Jo** had one such boss. She didn't put him in that position–management did.

Jo always did more than a great job and more than her share. She had several bosses who were fine men, but she had one who wasn't carrying his load and wouldn't try to change. **Jo** didn't like it when anything was wrong in her department and this man's actions were affecting several people under him. These people did their jobs as **Jo** did, but only **Jo** was in a position where she could let this man know he was not carrying out his responsibility. On one occasion, he told her he would be touring a new factory. In a series of telling phone calls, **Jo** got a call from that factory asking why he hadn't shown up. Another call told her he was staying at a fancy golf facility.

When he returned to the office, he had a very good suntan, one you couldn't get touring the inside of a plant, he had lied about where he had been. **Jo** closed the office door and told him how his suntan gave him away. She suggested that for the next plant he toured he should wait till the roof was up. From that day on, he did a better job until he was replaced a few months later.

Jo said she would never forget the look on his face when he had lied and knew he had been found out – how degrading and shameful it was for him to feel those kinds of feelings! **Jo** always wanted everything better and nobody hurt. She couldn't walk away from this situation, so she did what was right for all the people under him. **Jo** was honest, fair, friendly, and truthful. **Remember my Jo**.

Vacuum Sweeper

Jo was always wanting things cleaner. The vacuum sweeper was the answer most of the time, but she used the dustbuster a couple times a day for little pickups. She even bought dustbusters for gifts, because she felt they could help anyone in a pinch. I would buy **Jo** the strongest vacuum I could get and tell her she could clean with less effort and make fewer passes across the carpet, but she would still take near the same time and as many sweeps as before. She would say, "I know what I'm doing, Ken. Men don't know how to clean." I was always so proud of anything **Jo** did, because it was done so well.

When I heard that the Rainbow Sweeper was the best vacuum, I found out through the family that our niece, Denise, had a friend who was selling them. We had them come to our home to demonstrate it one night. **Jo** felt it was too expensive, but when I heard her say that, I ordered one quick. I knew **Jo** would know how much I loved her if I bought her the best.

She would get out one of her bigger sweepers at least once a week. I would say, " I'm leaving for outside now," which was our code for "you should use it, but not with me around." If she was using the Rainbow Sweeper, I would help put in the water, get it set up to use, and carry it to the room she was going to clean. **Jo** would then say, "I'll do it from here, Ken. You just go outside for awhile."

I told her it was the noise I couldn't stand, but that was just an excuse. Only one person could operate the sweeper at a time and she wanted to be the one. I didn't like her working hard when I couldn't help her. I couldn't talk to her either, while the vacuum was running and so I ended up just being in the way. If I couldn't help **Jo** it made me nervous, so I went outside. I never went far, usually just the garage to tinker, and was always at the ready to assist her if she needed me.

During these years, **Jo** and I were both working hard and our time at home was always rushed. One day she came home from work and told me that some of the women she worked with had a woman in to clean their houses once a week. I told her we could afford anything she wanted, so she hired a very nice lady to clean for us. This woman would clean one room of the house very well and give the rest a once-over each week. It was working out fine, our dog liked her, **Jo** could see progress and we had a new friend, but you've already guessed it, haven't you? **Jo** would clean the house each night before Mary would arrive. It still needed a little more cleaning, so Mary had something to do, but **Jo** couldn't back off completely. Mary was still a big help, so it was another win-win situation. Life can be so nice at times. **Jo** was so marvelous, I wanted her to have anything that would help her. When **Jo** was happy, I was happy. It was such a delight to be around her.

Up North

We spent a lot of time the last eight years with Chuck and Irene at their home near Clare. It was always up to Chuck and Irene to decide when we would go up North, because they were still running their company. They tried to spend the weekends up North, but that didn't always work out. When we were going there, **Jo** would have her hair done at a special time. Her hairdresser, who owned the shop, would always see that **Jo** was well taken care of. He cared a great deal about **Jo**; I think he knew she was my angel.

Chuck and I liked to eat at a place called, "Big Al's." **Jo** and Irene liked some other places nearby better because of their fish dinners, so we would sometimes drop them off and pick them up later. I didn't like seafood and **Jo** did, so she would go off with Irene. When we did eat together at "Big Al's," **Jo** and I enjoyed and commented on the decor. They had an old jukebox, an antique gasoline pump, movie posters of Clark Gable, Marlyn Monroe, Elvis and lots more

memorabilia. It was neat and very clean; they served great meals consisting of a salad bar, special breads, and great soups. Everything was very nice, but I always liked it even more when I was with **Jo**.

After eating, we would shop in town at a supermarket and a drug store for any items that we might need that week. A trip into town was mainly for shopping. **Jo** and Irene loved to shop, and Chuck liked it more than I did. Most people would say this was not very exciting, but for me it was joy because of my **Jo**. Her presence was all I needed. Her smile, her laugh, and her voice were the whole of my life. Sometimes Irene and Chuck's dog, Shannon, was with us; she always made up her own mind. I always had dogs that came when I called, always wanting to be with me, but Shannon would come one time, not the next. She would just go and lay down, having a mind of her own.

Most nights we enjoyed that wonderful game of cards called pinochle. In our card game, **Jo** and Irene were partners most of the time, wanting to show that women could win against the men they had married. Irene was a very Machiavellian player, but **Jo**, always a devout personage, wanted to make the most of anything she did. I think Chuck will admit that he always had his mind on something else entirely. I was attentive and kept score, because I knew that **Jo** would, as we prepared for bed, ask that wonderful question, "Did I do good, Ken?" It tickled me that she was concerned enough to ask me, when she and Irene customarily won most of the games. Her being interested even after playing thousands of games was a wonder to me. Later in the evening, we would watch a little television. Out of the corner of our eyes, we would watch for deer across the creek. If the deer appeared, we quickly turned on the yard lights and videotaped them. I have a lot of these tapes and review them now and then, enjoying my memories of those sweet times.

I liked to tease **Jo** and say she was cheating, because she was right-handed except when dealing cards. Those pretty hands, fingernails always done so beautifully, firing the cards out like a professional casino dealer. When I teased her, she would say, "Aw, Ken," with that little laugh, that I so longed to hear. If you are a pinochle player, you know how seldom it's likely you can take all the tricks. Whenever she did, she was thrilled, like she had just won a gold medal for the U. S. Olympic team. Not an outbreak of joy, but self- satisfaction. "I know I did good, Ken," was what I would see in those pretty blue eyes. "God," I pray, "let me see those blue eyes again."

Chuck has a pole barn full of his toys – working machinery, 3 and 4- wheelers, snowmobiles and, his latest purchase, a mule-4 wheeler that looks something like a golf cart. It's a wonderful cart for their property. **Jo** was always eager for a new experience, so she learned to drive it; I have a video of **Jo** and Irene racing around on the road in it, laughing and having a great time. If you see it, look at the size of **Jo's** smile.

When you have two homes to look after it can be very labor intensive. If you have the work done by others, it's seldom as good as you would have done yourself. Chuck and Irene are both very good workers and it is hard to get someone who will work like they do. Starting the pumps to water the lawn and keeping the lawn mowers running were jobs Chuck loved to do. He loved to operate his new riding lawn mower. He helped **Jo** operate it one day and I have a video tape of this, too. She did a good job. Chuck always kept the paths clear to the deer feeding stations where he installed automatic feeders that set out

feed a couple of times a day. We loved to walk and ride in the woods taking video photos that I now cherish.

Chuck always liked to cut up, constantly hollering things to get your attention. One day in the fall **Jo**, Irene, and I were raking leaves and hauling them to a special place, when Chuck rushed out of the pole barn hollering, "fire, Ken, fire, Ken." I'm thinking I'm not doing a good enough job and he's telling the ladies to fire me. He should have shouted, "Water," because his new lawn mower was on fire and he had nothing with which to put the fire out.

Suddenly realizing what was really happening; we sprang into action. We looked like the Keystone Cops. Irene ran for the house and **Jo** ran to Chuck to see what she could do. The pumps for watering the lawn weren't hooked up, and that would have taken several minutes, so I seized a bucket from the garage and raced for the stream to dip out some water. I got the bucket full of water only to see it running out on the ground; the hunters had shot the bucket full of holes! I ran back to the garage for a good bucket, filled it, and headed up the hill to the pole barn. Chuck had tried to put the fire out by smothering it, but that hadn't worked. The flames only shot higher! Water was the only answer. A lot of damage was done to the new mower before we had the fire safely out. Chuck called an engine repair shop and got the mower in to be fixed; I don't know what it cost, but I'm sure it was plenty. Chuck and Irene swore they'd put a fire extinguisher in the pole- barn, the garage, and the house, as well as a couple of buckets of sand in several different locations.

The day we were cleaning up
a fire starting did interrupt
All of us rushing into action
assisting each other was satisfaction
Nothing was planned or organized
pulling together was no surprise
Looking back we showed no class
no one hurt, we could still laugh
That night we played our pinochle game
talked of the fire and quenching the flame
This simple ending of the day
so happy it was ending this way
For me any night I could be with Jo
was a blissful fulfillment, I'm sure you know.

Practical

All the people who cared about me instructed me to be practical. We on Earth should look carefully into everything we do. Money matters should be carefully looked at; all situations, circumstances, and positions you find yourself in, should be scrutinized in order to be practical. However, I couldn't be practical with the love I had for my **Jo**, Mother, Dad and God. I honored them by not being practical. I'm asking God now to let me be with my **Jo**, so I can live again, and this time, nothing bad will happen.

I write about how life on Earth was marvelous for the brief time that the four of us were together. God gave us that moment of Heaven on Earth. Mother passed first and we continued on, because God willed it. Dad went on as long as he could, celebrating his God with the Bible always in his hand. If you think about the kind of people Mother and Dad were, you know they are in Heaven together enjoying the true love I celebrate in these stories.

Jo was my role model, the one person I loved over every other. No person who loves wants that loved one to suffer for even a second here on Earth. When my **Jo** started hurting, I wanted to take on her hurt, so I could hang on to her. I desired all the hurt, but **Jo** wouldn't let me have it. When it got to be too much for her, I had to let her go. I was numb and so mixed-up, because I had to let go of my Angel. Writing "**Remember my Jo**" is the reason I'm still on Earth.

On Earth you are tested for that better place called Heaven. If you live as Mother, Dad and **Jo** did, you will enter the Kingdom of Heaven as they did. When disease or accident or old age happens, God's calling is final. If you have lived as he wished, you will be with all good people when you pass from this life. The nuns at **Jo's** church told me that if you, the reader, will **remember my Jo**, I can be with my family again.

When young, you think life is forever
a big concern is simply the weather
You're a little older, the time slips away
the years rush by in just a few days
Still for you, it just hasn't sunk in
the wonders on earth will come to an end
On this planet you're never sure
in heaven you will be forever secure
When God unites us together again
it will forever and ever be Jo and Ken

Jo and Her '96 Sebring

Jo and I were driving near the Birmingham Chrysler-Plymouth dealership in our '87 LeBaron when I tried the horn. I told **Jo** the horn didn't work, and for safety reasons, I better get it fixed now. I pulled into the dealership and said to her, "Why don't you go look at the new cars while I have them write this up." She had been in the show room a very short time when she rushed back. "Ken, you have got to see this car!" she said. "If you like, order it," I said. She said, "I like it." When I joined her, she was ordering the new Sebring from Dennis. In a few minutes a mechanic came in and told me, "Your horn is working fine – no charge." Dennis, our salesman, asked, "Do you want to cancel the order?" I told him, "No way! I want **Jo** to have her wish – this new Sebring."

Our '87 LeBaron was eight years old with 34,000 miles on it – just broken in, but because **Jo** took such good care of it, you wouldn't know it had been out of the show room. **Jo** and I had agreed that if

something served us well, we would put it out to pasture. The LeBaron had served us very well. Fourteen people wanted it and the first one who drove it, bought it.

Jo *took such good care of everything – me, our home, her clothing, and all our possessions large or small. We always had everything nice because of her. When a man has a wonderful wife like* ***Jo****, it becomes easy to have what you want out of life.* ***Jo*** *was so good that I always wanted to do more for her. I know in my heart that having* ***Jo*** *for my wife for over 50 years made me very happy and any success I had was because of her.*

We had good friends and good people dealing with us, because when ***Jo*** *was involved, her appearance and her approach were so nice that anyone dealing with us wanted to please her. When* ***Jo*** *walked in a room, she showed her light-up personality. She couldn't just browse in a store, because people always came up to her. She had a wonderful effect on strangers and it didn't take long for them to be friends with us. She was so nice it had to be contagious. You would be a better person for being around* ***Jo****.*

Our salespeople, Dennis, and Jane, who also worked in new-car sales, became good friends of ours. ***Jo*** *had our cars serviced for over 30 years at Birmingham Chrysler-Plymouth. She had many good friends at the dealership who were very good to us.*

With my wonderful Jo around
I seldom touched the ground
I was always on the move
what can I improve?
Trying each day
to find an easy way
To make Jo's life
have less strife
Making sure her car
could take her as far
As she would need to go
nothing's too good for my Jo
Music always playing
that goes without saying
Jo loved it soft and low
it gave her such a glow
Her smile I can't describe
it was so soft and yet alive
I never saw her frown
Jo wouldn't allow one around.

God created all of us, but ***Jo*** *was special to me. If I could have created the perfect person for me, it would have been* ***Jo****. I thank God every day for the over 50 years I had with my wonderful* ***Jo****.*

Jo Helen Sharon and Bob

It was during WW 11 that Helen, Jo's mother, married Mike and gave birth to Robert, who always answered to the name Bobby. Sharon was born two years later. Having raised two young girls, Jo and Irene, Helen now had a second family in Bobby and Sharon. Just when her older girls were leaving the nest.

Discovering that Bobby was mentally challenged was a shock to everyone, but God works in mysterious ways. Jo helped in any way she could and this brought her in daily contact with her mother and her young family. He had to be supervised 24 hour's a day. He could dress with help and walk, but couldn't make decisions on his own. He could understand when spoken to, but wasn't able to talk for himself. Helen was a remarkable woman doing a superior job of an awesome task. Sharon, growing up with Bobby, assisted in any way she could. Many people who see how Sharon takes care of Bobby often remark that she has to be a saint, because she sure has the patience of one.

Sharon attended college where she made very high marks and received a degree. She was flown to New York for her interview with the J.C. Penny Company. It was a whirlwind accomplishment and she had a decade of storybook adventures with the company, first in the "Big Apple" and then in sunny California. ***Jo*** *was in touch via the telephone with her at least an hour each week.* ***Jo*** *loved the phone and communicating with her family.*

Whenever Bobby came to our house, he would play with the dog and then spend hours with the player piano. Bobby couldn't talk, but he would sing along with the player piano by the hour. We have tapes of the music that he loved – Elvis's songs were his favorites. ***Jo*** *and I, along with the rest of the family, would sit with him while he played. It was joyous for all that participated.*

After Mike retired, Sharon moved her parents and Bobby to a large, beautiful new home in the hills of California. Sharon always had new cars, T.V's, VCR's and the best furniture. Bobby, too, only received the best of everything. Oh yes, she got him his own player piano. He traveled well, and with a few small rewards, such as snacks would mind Sharon most of the time. Sharon took him everywhere – to church, to the shopping mall, and to visit the doctor's office, which he liked.

In California, Bobby attended school about five hours a day. The school secured a job at Carl's restaurant, two supervised hours each day, which was Bobby's pride and joy. He rode a local bus to work, never knowing that the driver was watching out for him, making sure he was O.K. It was a regular bus, but the driver looked out for certain people who needed help. It was a wonderful plan that helped the family a great deal. ***Jo*** *and I went to Carl's once and took pictures of Bobby at work without him knowing. We saw the joy he had interacting with the other* employees. They acknowledged him with a friendly, "Hi, Bobby," and that thrilled him every time. There are some wonderful, loving people here on earth.

After her parents passed away Sharon tried to keep working, but couldn't get the kind of reliable help that Bobby needed. Devoting so much of her life to Bobby, she could not now trust his care to the ones she hired who had proven over and over again that they were not worthy of her trust. Taking an early retirement was not what she wanted, but she saw no other alternative. **Jo** and I told her to do the best she could and that we would always be ready to help whenever we were called upon.

Bobby was always treated wonderfully by our family. He let us know he loved us by repeating our names over and over again. "**Jo**, **Jo**, I, I, (that was Irene,) Chuck, Chuck, Mark, Mark, Den, Den, Ken, Ken, Mommy, Mommy, Daddy, Daddy;" we would never know why he would want to repeat. We had no clue as to what would set him off, using someone's name for a month at a time, but he would stop repeating names if you told him to. He liked all the Holidays and Sharon never failed to get out his treasures for each, which was a full-time job in and of itself.

Jo devoted part of her life to helping Helen, Sharon and Bobby in any way she could. If they couldn't get something in California, they could call **Jo** and she would search it out and send it to them. She encouraged others to help, but if they forgot or couldn't, she was sure to fill the void. **Jo** is with her Mother now in Heaven preparing a place for the good people they loved who will eagerly join them one day.

Jo was There

*One night I went to bed about 11 p.m. I woke up suddenly at 3 a.m., feeling sick. I rushed into the bathroom and fell, laying there helplessly until **Jo** called the police. They, along with **Jo**, helped get me to the hospital. **Jo** rushed around doing everything for me; everytime I looked up, she was there. I needed her 4 different times that night and she was always there. Now my mind travels back through time ...*

Joan's house was flooded from a huge storm, the basement was full of water, a lifetime of items was being lost – Jo was there.
A truck pulled out in front of us and we were moving at 110 mph – Jo was there.
I was in another hospital and wanted out – Jo was there.
Marietta needed help – Jo was there.
Dad needed help, he was afraid he wouldn't survive – Jo was there.
Carrey needed help – Jo was there.
Two other occasions; I won't name names – Jo was there.
Barb and Tom needed help – Jo was there.
I saw my Mother cry only once – Jo was there, always helping in any way she could.

*When **Jo's** mother was moving from Michigan to California, an unbelievable amount of things had to be done in a very short time. We could not see this happening; there was just no way, but it was done, because **Jo** was there. How did she do it? **Jo** wasn't a doctor or a nurse nor did she have any special training. I look back and understand how she assisted everyone she could and did more than I ever-believed possible. It was because **Jo** was my Angel.*

***Jo** received so much gratitude in life, that only she, and God and I know about, because of her unending kindness to family and friends.*

Whenever I asked her why she was so nice, she said, "Aw, Ken," with that little laugh of hers that I always loved to hear.

Daisy and Bert

My Aunt Daisy, one of my mother's sisters, was a wonderful lady. Her husband, Bert, was a big man, well over 6 ft. tall and resembled John Wayne; you always felt safe with Bert around. They went out whenever they could. For Mother, Dad, Daisy and Bert, dancing was the big entertainment in those days. They were good dancers and enjoyed each other's company.

My mother was tied down with the responsibility of the six-day operation of her business and couldn't travel much, so she couldn't see the out-of-town relations. Daisy was the link to those relatives. She would visit, and in turn, invite the relatives to her home in Garden City. Daisy always brought them to see our home. This was great for us and we always had a good time.

Uncle Bert was a very hard worker and did an exceptional job at whatever his task was. He won a lot of prizes at the trucking company where he was a driver. If he promised you something, you could count on it. He was known to exaggerate, but we did not often call him on his exaggerations; the bigger the story he told, the more likely it was true!

Once, when we returning from a trip to see my Dad, who lived in Ohio, we were 200 miles from home on a small country road. Bert said, "I'm looking for a mom and pop store that has the best apples you have ever tasted." I was thinking, "a store out here in "no man's land," yeah, sure." A couple miles up the road, he pulled into the store he had so vividly described; I went in with him and the owners greeted him with open arms, so happy they were to see him again. They carried out a basket of the best apples we had ever tasted. Uncle Bert was proven right once again!

Daisy took to **Jo** *from the start, almost embarrassing us with the praise she had for* **Jo**. *Both Daisy and Bert loved* **Jo**; *they instinctively knew that this was a person they wanted to be close to. It only happened a few times, but when we needed them, they came through for us. In this life, you need an Aunt Daisy and Uncle Bert. We loved them very much.*

Barb and Tom

Tom, a cousin of **Jo's**, was a bit on the rough side as a young man and we didn't move at his pace. It wasn't until he was married for about 20 years that we found him to be moving at a pace we could enjoy. Barb, his wife, was always so delightful and we liked her from day one. I enjoyed Tom's dad, Joe, too. The stories him and Tom told were full of the kind of excitement we could appreciate from a safe distance.

At one time, Tom was having problems with a job and **Jo** stepped in and helped. **Jo** always tried to help without anyone knowing she had. Tom had been a barber, and when **Jo** heard he was out of work, she asked me to get in touch with him and ask if he would cut my hair. I did and he did. It was a quiet way to get money in his pocket without him feeling beholden.

In their later years, both Barb and Tom became diabetic. It was *very sad. Tom was on dialysis and lost one leg, then the other. Barb had back problems and respiratory disease. Their daughters and son helped them all they could. I don't understand why these things have to happen, but Tom became stronger as a result and a truly remarkable person at the end of his life. They both loved* **Jo** *very much and were grateful for her love for them. Tom had a rough start, but* **Jo** *was so proud when he turned out to be a good man. As you know,* **Jo** *always loved progress.*

If one of the men in the family was in the hospital, **Jo** *would ask me to call and cheer them up. I would do anything* **Jo** *wanted; she taught me how to care about people. Once I asked Tom to get me a man's hand hairdryer, which he did. When Tom was in the hospital, fifteen years later, I called and asked if that drier was still under warranty. He laughed so hard at this that I got great joy out of it. A couple years later, he was in the hospital again with diabetic complications, so I called. In an effort to keep the conversation light, I told him I hoped he would run over to see* **Jo** *and me as soon as he was able. " Ken, I'll only be able to hop over," he said, "they took off one of my legs." I felt so bad at what I'd unintentionally said that I quickly apologized and humbly hung up. I told* **Jo** *and we both cried, thinking of Tom's pain.* **Jo** *told me how bad she felt at hearing the news and that she was sure Tom knew I was only trying to help. She never told me anything that wasn't true. It's my belief that we will all happily meet in heaven where there will be no more hurting or sorrow, only eternal good times.*

Plantrich's Barbecue

In August Jo's nephew, Mark, and his wife Kris, have the annual barbecue that they are famous for. I have videotapes of this event from the past several years that we attended. If Jo were still here, we would have been excited about this wonderful day and the joy we would share. **Jo** would have had her hair done and she would have carefully chosen our clothes for this family-and-friends get together. The Sebring would have been clean, music would have been playing, and I would have been making the popcorn in the popcorn machine in our recreation room.

Jo has missed two of them now; she was the star of the event as far as I was concerned. I can no longer attend when my Angel is not with me. Life was so wonderful with my **Jo**, but now that's over. Still, I am glad for all those who can enjoy that wonderful day as before. More than five hundred people will have the joy that **Jo** and I experienced there together.

Kris and Mark will make it all possible. They go day and night preparing what is needed. The food is always marvelous, the fireworks tremendous and the horseshoe pits will be ready. There will be archery, fishing, and golf with a prize for "nearest to a – hole – in – one," as well as frisbee, baseball and basketball. Children, almost one hundred of them, will be having such fun in the sun, racing around a play yard and swimming in the pool. Kris has gardens with beautiful flowers, grapevines and two ponds for those who enjoy nature walks. For the younger adults, there will be a band playing over the loudspeaker system, dinner at 6 p.m. and fireworks around 9 p.m.

There is plenty of room for everyone. Some families come in campers and stay overnight. You're tired when you get home, but during the course of the day you have met with your old friends and made some new ones. Kris and Mark know how to have good clean fun; ***Jo*** *always liked that and I am sure she is watching. I hope someday soon that I can watch it from above with my* ***Jo****. Then we can relive those wonderful days all over again in slow motion, taking the time to smell the roses and to thank all those wonderful people.* ***Jo*** *loved life so much; God blesses my* ***Jo*** *and the people who knew her.*

Carrey

When the Roberts boys were suddenly orphaned in their childhood, they were split up, each going to a different home. Dad got a bad man who overworked and beat him. When Dad couldn't take it anymore, he ran away. Carrey, one of his younger brothers, stayed in farm country most of his life. "Cotton," as he was called, always needed help, so Dad looked after him as best he could at a distance, always worried about how he was doing. Dad tried to get him a better job in the city, but Carrey liked the outdoors.

I was a small boy when I first saw "Cotton." He was a small man, but wiry and an excellent worker. Lacking a formal education, he did hard farm labor and delighted in showing off how strong he was. He entertained people with a few tricks he excelled at, such as standing on his head or doing feats of physical strength that most larger men couldn't manage.

One day Dad received an urgent call from one of the local farmers who said Carrey needed help. Dad said that we should make a trip to see Carrey and do what ever we could. We found him living in an old, uninhabited farmhouse that was beyond repair. Jo was heartsick that we hadn't gotten to him before it had come to this. The local doctor said Carrey could travel back to Michigan with us, but would still need a lot of care.

We got him home safely where he saw Dad's Doctor, who recommended an immediate operation. After he was released from the hospital, **Jo** took good care of him in our home and he bounced back to health rather quickly. Chrysler was always looking for good workers, so Dad got Carrey a job there. I was working at the same plant, so Carrey rode in every morning with me. He was given a job that he really liked and Mr. Burke, his plant superintendent, told me he was a extraordinary worker and that he liked Carrey very much. Burke was superintendent over several hundred men, so that was quite a compliment. Carrey Roberts had a good life after a very painful, stormy start, because of the love his brother showed him.

Whenever I asked Cotton why he wasn't married, he said, "you need a bird house before you get a bird." He eventually bought two houses and then got married to a nice lady. She already had several grown children who took to Carrey right from the start. Carrey ended up retiring from Chrysler Corporation. He made a good profit, too, on his properties when he sold out in Michigan and moved to Missouri; he was a good old boy who always loved farm country.

We all loved Cotton for his independence and the joy he gave to others. He was a little man who was very strong, who gave much more than an honest days work for his pay. For all his small size, he was a big man. God loves him and so did we. Dad had worked his magic again and **Jo**, as well, had done more than her share.

One Day at a Time

I'm told that **Jo** wouldn't want me to be unhappy since her passing. I've heard people who mean well say that I have to get on with my life. Something is wrong with that thinking. My life was **Jo**; she told me her life was Ken. God knows we belong together forever and that will come to pass; our love is forever and ever. My life with **Jo** was full, it is empty now. Most of my time, day and night, is spent talking endlessly to **Jo** in my mind, asking her to help me to be with her. It won't be for much longer.

I try to remember special things to write about **Jo**. I ask for her help in doing this. This book proves I want to tell what joy I had and how I wish it hadn't ended. You know I want more that ever to be with her. I want a new beginning with **Jo**, Mother and Dad, all in slow motion. When I throw **Jo** a kiss now, I tell her she owes me one; the first thing I want to do in heaven is to collect all those kisses.

I wake up and say," I love you, **Jo**;" another one day at a time has started. The last thing I say at night is, "I love you, **Jo**." In between, I say her name over and over. Coffee first thing, newspaper and television, but no **Jo**. If God would only surprise me. My thoughts turn to flowers like never before and you know why.

Each day I collect the mail about noon; if there are any bills, I post them. I think about having a snack, but it won't have any taste. **Jo** and I always had great plans; without **Jo** I have no plans, it's just another one day at a time. It was so good for so long and now nothing matters anymore. **Jo** always added such a beautiful touch to my life. I get to see everything **Jo** had her hands in. I always check the basement and the pictures I have of her all through the house. I tell her how much I love her and want to be with her. We had it so good that talking with

Jo is serenity to me. Looking at things like arrows, and each thing she touched, is how I get by one day at a time.

It would have been even sadder if we hadn't had so much love and joy, always planning and caring for each other. Our love grew stronger everyday. Now I look at her pictures, listen to her voice, read her letters, and watch videotapes of her. I drive her Sebring and Imperial cars, write about her, and ask for God's help; it gets me by, one day at a time.

She was my life for so many years and the love we had was astonishing. Her desire to live as we always had, including the last few days she spent on earth when she was in such pain was heart breaking. **Jo** asked me to take her home and get her well. I tried, but she was hurting too much. "Please, God," I pray, "give me another chance to be with my **Jo**. I know we will be so happy once we are together again. Till then, I will get by, one day at a time."

You learn so much about your life
when it's almost over
Working and playing day and night
has put you in the clover
When you are sure you have made it,
the time here on earth runs out
You have so much to leave behind,
you wonder what this was all about
Jo and I enjoyed so much love
and felt we would have time for so much more
When some incompetent doctors
suddenly slammed that door

Living as Things Ought to Be

Not having a tape deck for our car radio, we would sometimes listen to Rush Limbaugh as we drove up North. I purchased his book; it was hidden in the bookstore, just as he had said it would be. **Jo** lived the life Rush advocated " – the way things ought to be." She felt a secure childhood, a good education, and a job had to come first in life. Start low, and then set your goals to make yourself happy in this life with comfort and love. **Jo** wanted to be an executive secretary, a very fine goal, and she met it. Her teachers had all directed her to that position as they saw she would excel at it.

I loved to see her sign her name; it reminded me of that old-time comedian sitting down to play the piano. She would look at her hands, sit very upright and flex her fingers a few times, place the pen or pencil just right in her hand and begin to write, "**Jo Roberts**," then she'd stop to look at it with satisfaction. She sought perfection at each job she did. I could always count on **Jo** as everyone could. I would go to her with questions about spelling and she always had the correct answer. She out-spelled me every time. She even made me feel good that I had asked her. That was **Jo's** way.

Jo had to initial all her work at Chrysler; using "jr" made all her bosses juniors, so they had her sign her own name, "**jo**," to everything she did. She enjoyed the name "**jo**" and no work went out without it. She always desired to do a very neat and beautiful job. Everyone whom she worked for had praise for her work. You knew it was **Jo's** work; no one had to tell you. She was rightfully very proud of what she produced.

She made friends wherever she went. The cafeteria people at the Chrysler plant knew and liked her. The employees of restaurants near *the plant felt the same as well. Even when purchasing her clothing the salespeople looked out for her, putting special things away for her approval. I saw this whenever I shopped with her. She did not seek out these attentions; people just always wanted to help my* ***Jo****. When you are a loving, caring person like* ***Jo****, no one rushes up to you; instead they become aware of your presence gently.* ***Jo*** *put out so much love it will keep coming back forever and ever. Something good will always reward all that practice this. Remember* ***Jo*** *and her presence of love.*

Till we meet again

I can see now that my whole life was lived in the spirit of " till we meet again;" I was always looking forward to seeing **Jo**. My final journey is to see **Jo**, so I am writing this book now in the sprit of " till we meet again." A nun told me that when people are able to read "**Remember my Jo**," I will be able to meet **Jo** in Heaven. You know that I believe **Jo** was my Angel here on Earth. She guided me from the day we met. I always thank God for giving me to Mother and Dad and then the three of us coming to love and appreciate **Jo**. I can't say enough about the love they showered on **Jo** and me. I am repeating myself, but I have so much love for them still. **Jo** was always my honey.

Jo was so proud of our name, Roberts; she knew that Dad and Mother honored our name and pledged that we would, too. We always paid our bills, honored our handshake, and any contract we made, never making a promise we didn't keep. We always tried to leave a place cleaner than we found it, too. I don't have to tell you about **Jo** and clean. She said her mother, Helen, always told her, " cleanliness was next to Godliness."

I try to carry on with my life, but I am so lost without **Jo**. She was my life and such an enchantment. Each time we parted, even if it was just her leaving my line of sight, it was "till we meet again." I hope you have someone like my **Jo** to love and love you. If you find the one person for you, you can share a wonderful life making this world a better place together. I believe we are at liberty to do good or bad, but it has been my belief that everyone coming into this world has God wanting them to obey the dictates of the Bible. With Mother, Dad, and then **Jo**, I always wanted to honor them and be the best person I could. It will never change for me. I will **remember my Jo** "till we meet again."

Aunt Ollie

Jo always enjoyed entertaining the relatives on my side of the family and Aunt Ollie was one of her favorites. Aunt Daisy would keep us up to date about Ollie's life. "As a young girl, she was a real beauty," Aunt Daisy said, "almost as pretty as **Jo**." I'd heard that she had four or five husbands. Aunt Ollie had a pass to travel on the railroad, so we looked forward to meeting her. She was staying with Daisy and Bert on a short visit and Bert told us we were in for a treat. "Ollie, although up in years, is a real firecracker," he said, "and she has a mind like a steel trap." He didn't exaggerate at all this time. She was over 75 and as sharp as a carpet tack.

Ollie had spent a lot of years campaigning for politicians, even assisting Truman in his bid for the presidency. She knew a lot of dignitaries in Kansas City and could talk for hours about them. She had been in the backrooms of politics and was very knowledgeable. What we learned from that lady was sometimes unbelievable, but she had been there. She gave names, dates, places and details that no one could have made up.

Uncle Bert told me privately that Ollie had become disillusioned with politics and life in general; she was bitter about politicians. Ollie had a backseat view and she saw how incompetent the leaders actually were. Still, she commanded our attention with her political stories, all of them fascinating. She had experienced a great deal and was a strongbox full of knowledge. She desired to share this with people she cared about, so it was always educational to be around her. One night Aunt Ollie, sitting at our "Cheers" bar, turned it into her podium. Our papers had run some rather sad stories about a flood that had just hit Kansas City and the surrounding areas. She said, "most of the people in those bottom lands that had been flooded deserved what they got; they built their homes on a natural flood plain and will be back to try again."

Aunt Daisy told us that Aunt Ollie was much more candid with her and Bert. She said that Aunt Ollie would literally put on an iron corset when she came to visit us. She knew ***Jo*** *was a lady and she wanted to make a good impression in front of her. Ollie was a real joy every time we saw her. She enjoyed music, stories, joking and her favorite subject – politics. When she passed* ***Jo*** *and I lost someone very special. She had shared a great deal with us. "We love you, Aunt Ollie."*

Victor Roberts

Victor Roberts, Dad's oldest brother, was a tall, slender man. He served in the Army during World War 1, seeing a lot of action, including contact with mustard gas, a powerful nerve poison. Upon his return home from the war, he married a nice young girl and they had three delightful daughters in as many years. Their problem was that he would vanish without a trace for years at a time. We never knew why he would leave his family without a word; some said it was war-related, probably due to the mustard gas attack. He would drink heavily to kill the recurring nerve pain he constantly suffered and lose his job, and then he'd vanish for long periods of time.

The story my mother told about Uncle Vic describes his situation best. Next door to Mother's first beauty shop was a grocery store. One day Mother gave Uncle Vic a twenty-dollar bill to go next door for change, so she could make change when her customers required it. When he didn't return that day or several days thereafter, Mother wrote on her calendar the exact date he had left with her twenty-dollar bill. Exactly two years to the day, Vic walked in and handed her a ten, a five, and five ones. He never said a word about being gone and neither did Mother. They both acted as if he were right on time.

Uncle Vic would show up on our doorstep from time to time, take as little asistance as he could from Dad, and always pay him back. Vic could always get a job as a night watchman, then rent a furnished room until he disappeared once more. He was never a hardship to us, always clean and neat, orderly and courteous. Dad tried to help him, but he said, "Alton, I don't want to disappoint you, but I know I won't stay long at any job."

Once he sent Dad a newspaper clipping reporting that "local man, Victor Roberts, an innocent by-stander, was shot in a bank holdup."

He wrote on the margin, " I dodged a lot of bullets in France, only to be shot outside a bank in Los Angeles." That was the last time my Dad ever heard from him.

I invited his only surviving daughter, Florence, to visit with me and she stayed for ten days. I hadn't seen her in sixty-five years. I told her that I felt her dad had some good qualities. "All I can remember of him," she replied, "is his not being there for us." Her mother and her sisters had all had a hard time of it, because of Uncle Vic's vanishing act. I couldn't walk in Uncle Vic's shoes, so I don't know what caused him to desert his family. I know he had some worthy qualities, but this question always haunted the family. I believe God will answer all questions, so **Jo** and I will ask. This is one of the mysteries we want solved.

What I Owe My Jo

We were born, and spent many years on earth, before credit cards showed up in our economy. I am happy to say I have only owed one person in the world – -that person was my **Jo**. I owed her because she did so much for me. I owed her, for all the letters she wrote, the love she gave me, the care she took of me, her visits during the war, the phone calls, the pictures she sent, the inspiration she was, and how she gave me the desire to be a caring person.

She told me, "when we marry, we will always be together and have a good life." She knew that nothing would stop me from marring her. It wasn't if, only when. We were that much in love, still we knew each other for 5 years before we married. Youth, and the war, you know.

Eventually we were both forced by market conditions to obtain credit cards, but we used them sparinglyand didn't abuse them. We worked hard and watched our money grow. If you had someone like **Jo**, you always had love and you could bank on that. I made some mistakes in my life, but I didn't' know of one that **Jo** made. I liked to invest the money we made; I'm not talking about a lot of money, but the amount was important to us. **Jo** was my associate in business and I wanted to be good to her. I made some money and lost some. **Jo** said, "I would like to try;" she picked only products she liked herself and I don't remember her having a loss.

We both had remarkable relations with the brokers we picked. We made it a rule that they had to come to our house and meet us. We ended up on a first name basis. I believe that the brokers, or anyone else **Jo** met, had special feelings for her and that was shared by me. If everyone lived like **Jo** did, this would be near Heaven on earth. We all become Monday morning quarterbacks **after** the game. That is what I am now. I still have a crush on my **Jo**.

Christmas with Jo

We had over 50 joyous Christmases together in all kinds of weather. I always put up the outside decorations with Jo's *help. The five Santa bears were set out. We put a huge stocking bear on the outside of the front door and Jo would fill it with boxes. She gave it that pretty touch. You had to see it to enjoy what Jo could do. In the recreation room, Jo helped me put up the garland, splashing silver, green, gold, and white all around. We had Christmas music playing most of the time from the carousel that Jo had purchased in California.*

We would put our Christmas tree in the Spa room and it looked so nice during the day with the freshly fallen snow outside. At night you got the reflections from the 20 windows and the skylight. It was a beautiful sight to behold.

Jo loved Christmas, because it was a clean holiday and a time to give; She always wanted to give. People were happy and everything looked so nice. We had over 50 years of ornaments, more lights than we knew what to do with. We had over 40 boxes of Christmas items to look at; we would actually use about half. Jo took such good care of everything; love and pride went into everything she would display.

Jo wrapped most of the presents, did most of the work, trimmed the tree a bit every day until Christmas. She always shopped and put a great deal of love in everything she did, thinking about each item she wrapped and what it would mean to the person receiving the gift. Jo always did more than her share. She did more for me than I did for her. As hard as I tried, I never could out do my Jo.

Denise had us over on Jo's last Christmas on earth. We had a joyous time and I have a short video of it. The memories of Jo stand out. She loved her mother, her church, her letters, her possessions, clothing, shoes, pocket-books, as well as her collections of hats, jewelry, candles, her assortment of clowns, cameras and the pictures she took. Jo loved everybody. I'm the only one who knew how much Jo loved life.

Jo lived by the Ten Commandments. I want everyone who knew Jo to pray that Jo and I will get together again in Heaven. I know that any time you could have spent with Jo and didn't was your loss. In her diary she cried for me and in her letters she

prayed for me and said she loved me more than I could ever know. I'm looking forward to eternity with my Jo.

Our minds are our recorders of things
of the past
I rewind and see Christmas with Jo –
what a blast
Jo's Christmas joy abounds each December
with her it was so nice, a great time to remember
Time reversed, seeing her is a pleasure
going back to be with Jo, my treasure.
I wonder what christmas in Heaven is like?
with Jo there now, it's a more beautiful sight
I'm sure she has improved everything she touched
others are enjoying what I now miss so much
I'll soon join her and my pain will dwindle
our love certainly will be rekindled
No more holiday days that I will agonize
with Jo I'll be rejoicing, because she's my prize.

Helen and Dick Chapman

Helen and Dick Chapman were good friends of ours. They lived across the street from **Jo's** sister, which is how we met. **Jo** and I visited them many times when they relocated near Port Hope in Northern Michigan. They, in turn, visited us in Bloomfield Hills several times. They or we could never stay long enough. **Jo** and I always felt Helen and Dick were very special people.

During one of their visits, they noticed some glass bowls we had sitting on a counter. They asked us where we had gotten them and did we know they were valuable? They told us the bowls were called "Carnival glass." We knew we liked them, but we didn't know they had any real value. Helen and Dick had been gathering glass collectibles for many years and brought us a book that showed that these were some very valuable period pieces.

*Many years ago when a Carnival came to town, this was one of the prizes that people could win. My Grandmother Anderson had given this glass to my mother, who in turn gave it to **Jo**. **Jo** had kept all the Carnival cups, bowls, and saucers to remind her of Leta, whom she had dearly loved. We had been using the bowls to hold change, keys, eyeglasses and miscellaneous papers, tossing them around in our everyday moves. I said, "maybe we should put them away," but **Jo** said, "nothing doing, they're a reminder of your mother and I want them out." I said, "**Jo**, you're right, I wasn't thinking. I know you will take as good care of them as mother had."*

*I know Grandma Anderson loved them. She had so few possessions that when she gave them to my Mother, it meant a great deal to both of them. I had often seen **Jo** wash them by hand – no dishwasher for this valuable Carnival collection. It was the memories **Jo** wanted to preserve as long as possible. Helen and Dick had brought these memories back to life for us and I thank them for it. Now the brightly colored Carnival glass reminds me of Mother and **Jo**. I hope to pass that memory along. Never put your memories away; cherish them every day of your life as I do now. It's a way of saying, "I love you." Grandma, mother and **Jo**, you know I do."*

Inflation

Returning to the United States from service during World War 11 and needing a new car meant you had to get in line. The car **Jo** *and I had would get us by for awhile longer, but spare parts for older cars were scarce. No new cars had been built for several years, so there was little to choose from. Everyone had to sign up to get their names on a waiting list. If you gave profiteers extra money on the Q.T., you could get one quicker; it was called "the black market."* **Jo** *and I decided to wait our turn.*

We purchased a six-cylinder, two-door Plymouth Club Coupe, Special Deluxe, equipped with radio, heater and white-sidewall tires. Our new car cost $1,250.00, but this was a fine automobile and we were very proud of it. **Jo** *and I were happy with its performance, too. We had wanted a convertible, but it was a full two years later before the automobile companies began manufacturing convertibles again. Sometimes you just can't get what you want and we had to accept this.*

Forty years later, **Jo** *and I paid the same amount of money, $1,250.00, for a two-wheel pushcart popcorn machine for our recreation room, proof of inflation eating away at our hard-earned money. I'm happy to say that our popcorn machine is valued at $2,000.00 today, but it's not for sale. Sharing and caring was always what* **Jo** *did all her life. She was someone on this earth who was very, very special.* **Jo** *and I always shared anything we had with others. We enjoyed making popcorn for each party we had and always supplied popcorn to many of our friends and neighbors. It was always our pleasure. All I want in return is that they remember my* **Jo**.

Did I do good, Ken?

In March of 1995, ***Jo's*** *shoulder and arm started giving her a little pain. She saw her doctor and started the treatment he prescribed. Taking her medicine and following the doctor's orders to the letter, she got better and was soon feeling great. We resumed everything without the slightest concern. She was herself again, smiling and flitting around as always.*

A year later, she once again began to feel more pain in the same shoulder and arm. The doctor again prescribed the same treatment, along with some physical therapy to be done at the Franklin Racket Club. ***Jo*** *was making good progress for a month, then suddenly one morning she couldn't get out of bed. At her request, I called her sister Irene, then phoned the doctor to get permission to take* ***Jo*** *to the hospital. He wanted* ***Jo*** *to come to his office, but after I told him of her condition, he agreed that it would be smart to get an ambulance and take her to the hospital. Irene rode in the ambulance with a very frightened* ***Jo****. I followed in* ***Jo's*** *Sebring thinking she should be home in a few days. "I'm sure with good treatment and the proper equipment this nightmare will be over," I thought, "and my* ***Jo*** *will be home very soon." That is why you go to a hospital, to get well. She told me she felt the same. Home in a couple of days was what we were both thinking.*

Jo *always asked me at the end of any special occasion – New Years, Easter, Thanksgiving, Christmas, any party or large get-together – "Did I do good, Ken?" I want to say to the world what I always told my angel* ***Jo****: "You did better than good, you were wonderful." She always made life such a pleasure everywhere she went.*

Having read about ***Jo****, I'm sure you will agree, earth was a better place while* ***Jo*** *was here. Now heaven is a better place. "Heaven is a* *better Place" are the words I had put on her monument. I will always be thankful for the life we had together on this earth and I look joyfully forward to our future. "**Remember My Jo**," as you move on with your life. "I know you love me, **Jo**," I say every night, "but I love you more. I'll soon prove it to you."*

Lady of the House

*When a friend or relative entered our home, **Jo** would always greet them with her beautiful smile, acknowledging them with a kind greeting and asking if they'd like something to eat or drink. It was her way of saying, "we hope you will have a good time here with us and will want to return."*

*Food is first on the list when entertaining guests and we had a good friend, Erick, who was always glad to help us. He owned a food service business a couple of miles from us. He was a caterer who catered to **Jo**. When we called him, he was always ready to make special dishes for us. Erick made a Hawaiian Chicken that was out of this world. He put* aside special cuts of meat for his special customers, one of whom was **Jo**. When we planned large parties, Erick would store items in his huge refrigerators for us. He was our good friend for many years and we enjoyed his company anytime he visited our home.

Jo wanted clean, neat, comfortable, and gratifying surroundings. She wanted to create a place where you could enjoy music, peaceful decor, and wholesome fun. **Jo** would not allow any profanity or unkind actions. It was meant that people of all ages would enjoy the time spent in our home. **Jo** enjoyed talking about the happy past and glorious future while sipping a coke as soft music was playing in the background. The memories of the good times we spent together are immeasurable. **Jo** was such a joy to be around. I wish you could have known her, but reading this book will help you know my Angel **Jo**.

When I enter the recreation room now, I have such wonderful memories of **Jo** – how she laughed and enjoyed so many hours with so many fine people. She made life worth living by always thinking of other's happiness first. Until the day I'm with her again I can only say, "I love you, **Jo**," always thinking of a phone call or a letter from heaven to our special phone booth or mailbox. **Jo** was my life on earth and soon I will be with her forever in heaven.

When Jo called my name

"Ken," I heard; it was **Jo's** voice. "**Jo,**" I said, not quite believing that it could be **Jo**. Still I didn't want to scare her away. "Ken," she called again "**Jo,**" I responded. We each repeated this several times. "Ken," – – – – - "**Jo,**" – – "Ken," – – – – – – "**Jo,**" – – – – - "**Jo,**" – - "Ken". I was so excited. I was pursuing the sound of her voice all through the house and then I saw her sitting on the dining room floor.

"Did you fall?" I asked.

"Yes", she answered.

"Are you hurt?"

"No, Ken".

I picked her up, held her in my arms for a long, long time; it felt so good. "**Jo** is here; she at no time went away. **Jo** is here, **Jo** is here," I thought as I was hugging her in my arms; I'm so happy that she's back and her leaving was only a sinister dream. My **Jo** is with me. The hugging lasted for a long time. Then as quick as her voice had arrived, she was no longer in my arms.

It's been over 15 months since **Jo** went away and I have asked for her presence each day and night. This is her first emergence and I now know she will come again. Until I am with her I will always keep looking. I want to thank God for what happened.

I waited many days to write about what happened, telling no one. I wanted the experience to duplicate itself; however, I'm sorry to say it hasn't. In review, **Jo** and I had a conversation; I asked, she answered – it was real communication. **Jo's** voice of 55 years answered. Her *marvelous voice was as always, so calm and so soft. I felt such joy hearing her and holding her in my arms. How did she get here? I don't care how. She was here. Her presence brought such indescribable joy. The joy I felt then is what I want to feel forever.*

Much later on April 8, 1998, 21 months to the day after ***Jo*** *passed away; I said my prayers, asking God to let me dream about* ***Jo****, as I had done every night. About 2 a.m. I woke up from the following dream:*

Jo *was chasing me around a dining room table. It was a very nice table with shiny, high-back chairs, made of a beautiful wood.* ***Jo*** *was pushing me ahead of her, until she pushed me into a corner. She was gently touching me; I was so happy feeling* ***Jo's*** *touch and presence. I have no idea how long this went on before I awoke.*

In real life I would be chasing ***Jo****, that's for sure. The only furniture that I could think of like the furniture in my dream was Mother's dining room set. She was so proud of the mahogany table with the high-back chairs.*

It has been seven months since the day ***Jo*** *called my name. When I asked the people at* ***Jo's*** *church how I could figure this out, I was told, "accept what God gives you." I always accept and thank God for anything that includes my* ***Jo****. I hope she is trying to keep in touch with me in any way she can. How can I not try to figure this out? Telling me to accept, but not to think, is impossible. I'm happy if I'm thinking about* ***Jo****. I'm sure both God and* ***Jo*** *want me to be happy. It's a* dilemma. I want my **Jo** to be my co-pilot and navigator as she always had been. I'm so happy whenever I feel **Jo's** presence, that I want more dreams like this one and I want to hear **Jo** call my name again.

Jo did everything with ease
her wanting so to please
So easy was her way to live
nothing stopped her wanting to give
The beauty and wonder of this world
was sampled and loved by this beautiful girl
She made everything such a gift
all who knew Jo were enriched.
It was a blissful fulfillment I'm sure you know
that came in the name of my marvelous Jo.

If you didn't give and receive love
during your time here on earth
You have wasted God's most wonderful
gift,
your singular and spectacular birth
Jo gave and rightfully received so much love
I know she is waiting for me in our special
paradise above
I was so blessed with Jo giving me her love.

Going on without Jo

There was no such thing as credit cards when **Jo** and I got married. If you wanted something, you had to pay for it then and there. The old saying was, "in God we trust, all others pay cash." During the Depression not even the banks had money. There were no loans available at any price. You needed money as collateral to get a loan and no one had any real money. Mother and Dad paid cash for everything they ever owned and they worked hard to earn their money.

World War 11 made it possible for a lot of people to secure employment. The people who had lived through the Great Depression jumped in and really put work at the top of the list. We were taught that work was very high on the list of most desirable things to do. Saving money, too, was seen as very important when you had been poor for a long time as most had been. Our name, a hand shake, meant a lot to us and the people we dealt with.

Jo's mother was a good provider. As a widow, she did very well raising her two daughters, but when **Jo** and I married she couldn't help us get established in life. My parents, wanting to help us save for a home of our own and the future, asked us to move into their new house on the East Side of Detroit.

Dad, being diabetic at such a young age, was our family's first cross to bear, but the sudden passing of my mother at the young age of 40 devastated us all. It was almost impossible to go on. Mother took so much of our love with her. **Jo** was the rock of strength that pulled Dad and I together and together we moved on. Dad put a lot of his energy into work and helping us get our own household established. Some year's later he married a woman who was a nurse, who loved him and took very good care of him. They lived a good life together and had a *son, my half-brother, whom they named David Joe. David Joe was a joy for all who knew him.*

Mom died then Dad and now ***Jo****. I couldn't write about this until near the end of this memoir because I don't like sadness. My life on earth, for all intents and purposes, ended with* ***Jo's*** *passing. I don't have* ***Jo*** *to go on with. I was told by some Catholic Sister's who attend, the church* ***Jo*** *always attended, that if people like what I've written and will say* ***Jo's*** *name and* ***remember my Jo,"it*** *will speed up my being with her. The church sisters told me that the book, "****Remember My Jo****" was what I had to give the world. Being with* ***Jo*** *is what I want again so please, "****Remember My Jo****," and help put us together, if you will, God will bless you, I know.*

From Ken to Jo

Jo Loved Life

*"I'm never going home, Ken," **Jo** said, lying helpless in her hospital bed. " I'll get you home, **Jo**," I said. "Ken, they're breaking me," she replied. The orderly taking her for a stand-up bath had dropped her on the hard tile floor, breaking her hip. This was her first stand-up bath since entering Beaumont Hospital. Two orderlies are required, but there had only been one. "I'm never going home, Ken, they are killing me," she cried. "I'll fix you, **Jo**, I'll get you home," I said. I knew she thought I could fix anything, but this I couldn't fix. **Jo** passed away in a few days, I don't remember how many. If I had slammed into a brick wall at full speed, I couldn't have hurt any more than I did. It was days before I really understood that long day; I still, at times, don't believe it. The loss of **Jo** was so terrible; the only reason I could stand the pain of our separation was knowing she was with God, and I had no other option. When I see **Jo** in heaven, I want to be able to fix her and bring her home as I promised. With God's help it will be done. **Jo** never broke a promise to me and I don't want to break one to her.*

*I would have given my life for **Jo**; and if she was going, I wanted to go with her. The last three days before she passed away, I could feel her strong desire to live and saw the pain it was causing her. I would have done anything to stop her pain. She meant the world to me. **Jo**, throughout our life together, had always given me so much pleasure; I couldn't think of life here on earth without her. Even now, I can't understand why my heart doesn't break.*

*The hospital **Jo** was in, I'm sorry to say, was not good to us. They left her waiting in a cold basement of the hospital for over four hours while a biopsy machine was being fixed; it wasn't to be fixed that day. Even before they dropped her, she had contracted pneumonia. What* *happened to her should not have happened, and they all know it.* ***Jo*** *would never have treated people the way she was treated. Not all were to blame, but it starts at the top and they wouldn't even talk to me when I was losing the most precious thing on earth. I hope the people who read "****Remember my Jo****," will not abuse the jobs they have. It brings me to the boiling point. I won't say anymore, I can't say anymore; it won't bring my precious* ***Jo*** *back to me.*

God had put us together over 50 years ago and had given us the chance to have so much happiness with each other. I had no idea that ***Jo*** *wouldn't be all right. I was lulled into thinking* ***Jo*** *and I wouldn't be separated for a second.* ***Jo*** *and I lived together and we wanted to die together. We loved each other that much.*

Conclusion

The priest who conducted **Jo** service asked me to write a few words he would read telling of a small part of **Jo's** life. I wrote the following for her service.

When **Jo** and I met, we were both teenagers. I fell in love with her the first time I saw her. We dated until I went into the service. I received more than a thousand letters from **Jo** while there. She got me through World War 11.

My mother loved **Jo** because of her beauty. My mother spent her life in her beauty salon. If my math is correct, **Jo** went to the beauty shop more that 4,000 times. **Jo** was as beautiful on the inside as she was on the outside. My mother loved **Jo** more and more each day. They got along well, shopped together; they did everything while I was in the service. My dad didn't take to **Jo** at first because they had different religions, but she soon won him over.

Jo retired from Chrysler Corporation as an Executive Secretary after nearly 30 years.

I can't think of one person who didn't like **Jo**. She was loving and loyal, honest, hard working, truthful and friendly. Her only fault was that she was too neat and too clean. I know she will do well in Heaven and Heaven will agree with her.

We always knew where the other one was at all times. On our 50th Wedding Anniversary, I said, "lets try for 50 more," and she quickly agreed. We were compatible in every way and in my next life I want to be with her. What greater tribute can I give to my **Jo**?

When **Jo** entered Heaven it became a better place. I want to be with her now.

All my love forever,
Ken

Jo

If you read my book
you've had a look
at what I was able to see
It was Jo a two letter word
that meant so much to me
Jo was all I had to know
that name would cause
our love to grow
I hope and I pray
that each day you'll say that
two-letter word Jo
From Ken to Jo and back again
Jo to Ken, love that will never end
As my wife
she became my life
Fifty years of bliss
sealed with her kiss
Jo wanted to give
it was her way to live
Her kindness and love
came from above
She brought it to earth
thank God for her birth
She asked God to bless me
Jo was so naive she didn't know
She was the blessing
God gave to me.

*My only desire now is to be with my **Jo**. Never being without her until now, I couldn't experience this feeling or express it. **Jo** has to realize how much I miss her and love her. God has to know I want to be with my **Jo** again as soon as possible. I do not know why it couldn't have lasted forever. The joy Dad must be having with Mother and **Jo** is the joy I'm looking forward to.*

*In this life with all its strife you need a
girlfriend who will stay to the end I couldn't
know her name would be Jo once we met how
could I forget All through the war letters
galore later my wife what a wonderful life I
traveled half the nation ending up with God's
magnificent creation,
Jo.*

Holding Jo's hand was a thrill forever
to touch Jo was such a pleasure
We walked hand in hand
that feeling was grand
The grip, the squeeze
she did so with ease
As we walked
if she talked
Always soft and low
by choice, the pace slow
I'd look at Jo and see
she was all-aglow for me

Jo came to Earth on a sunny day in June
a beautiful flower always in bloom
Bright was the glow I saw every day
it hurts so much now that she is away
A smile so special everyone knew
Jo presence; what a marvelous view
Her chair to the right of me, I give it a glance
I'm always hoping I'll see her by chance
That perfect face, fantastic hair
Oh! What I'd give if only she were there
Wanting to see or hear her soft voice
willing to bargain, please give me my choice.

Gold Star

They loved the person it represented
lost them to monsters corrupt
A gold star shines forever to
the people who put it up
This world can't give back to the families
that lost love ones in a war
with those they adore
Can't we ever learn what killing will do?
stop before it gets to me and you
Hurting in the world has
been such a horrible sin
Love is the only way
to bring it to an end
Heaven is the place where
those lost will be found
All good people will walk together
on holy hallowed ground.

Leta and Jo's Diary

I can't put into words what they had to say
loving family and country more each day
Coming out of the depression spirits low
then a war they knew would surly grow
They helped to put our country back piece by piece
conquering hard times, their efforts never ceased
Mom and Dad had just got on hurting feet
when the Japanese at Pearl Harbor sunk our fleet
The pain they felt they would not express
now the world is being covered with death
My wonderful Dad stood so very tall
showing his greatness through it all
Mother as always was up beat
always so strong on tired feet
Hardships defeated at any cost
making sure the world wasn't lost
Always writing sweet things to me
making sure that I wouldn't see
The sad burden with love, they carried each day
in the dairy's they had so thoughtfully put away.

Jo was Three

Ken was Four

Ken's Belated Wish
When I saw this picture of Jo

If I could have only met Jo
when she was three and I was four
we would have had thirteen years more
I think about that
it's not a fact
only God could take us back
Her dad would have sent me away
not allowing me to play
until a job I could sway
Peddling papers, I would land
making money, love is grand
Jo and I walking hand in hand
The love she left behind I'll bring to
her someday
It's a heavy load but not too much for
me to carry her way
I'm so looking forward to that joyous
wonderful day
She won't believe how much my love has grown
I added it without her knowing
I express it in secret even when she's above
God let's you do anything as long as it's
with love.

Somebody is watching over me

Jo is that somebody
who is watching over me
I look to the Heavens now
Someday I'll take a bow
Life here on Earth will end
joining Jo my wife and best friend
The happy life we once knew
I know that God will renew
Seeing Jo under Heavens marquee
waving and smiling as she comes to me
I've never heard of a soul breaking
I will give it a test that is love-shaking
"I love you, miss you, need you, Always
yours, if you want me,
Love, Kenney"

That's how I ended all my letters to Jo. That's how I'll end "Remember My Jo."

I would like to thank the following for ***Jo's*** *and my wonderful life.*

<u>Businesses</u>
Chrysler Corporation • Marathon • General Electric
Hudson's • Estee Lauder • London Fog • IBM
Microsoft • Dell • Mary Kay • Isotoner Totes
Hanes Ultra Sheer • RCA

<u>Church</u>
St. Owens

<u>Home</u>
Sarah Fisher

<u>Entertainers</u>
Wayne Newton • Frank Sinatra • Glen Miller
Willie Nelson • Elvis Presley • Nat King Cole
Reba McEntire • Randy Travis • The Judds

<u>Sports</u>
Jo's all time favorite football player from his early days
John Elway; she loved the way he scrambled.

Jo was 68 in the photo on page 246.